Decorative Art
and Modern Interiors

Studio Vista   London

William Morrow and Company, Inc. New York

Decorative Art
and Modern Interiors

Themes in Nature

volume 68

edited by Maria Schofield

Cover (front)
The recreation room in 'The "K" Villa on
Lake Yamanaka, Yamanashi Prefecture,
Japan'
architect: Shigeru Uchida
photography: Yoshio Shiratori

(back)
Sea-facing view of the 'Twin
Dunehouses at Atlantic Beach, Florida,
USA'
architect: William Morgan Architects
photography: Creative Photo Service

Title page
The stained glass windows in the
Church of St Marien, Bad Zwischenahn,
West Germany. The artist, Ludwig
Schaffrath, used only antique, clear and
white opal glass; natural light and the
trees outside provide colour that
changes with the seasons.
photography: Inge Bartholomé

A Studio Vista book first published in the UK in 1979 by
Cassell Ltd
35 Red Lion Square, London WC1R 4SG
and at Sydney, Auckland, Toronto, Johannesburg,
an affiliate of
Macmillan Publishing Co Inc
New York

Copyright © Studio Vista, a division
of Cassell Ltd 1979

Published in 1979 by William Morrow and Company, Inc
105 Madison Avenue, New York NY 10016, USA

Library of Congress Catalog Card Number 78–71658
U.S.ISBN 0–688–03480–2
U.K.ISBN 0–289–708–60–5

Designed by Gillian Riley
Set in Monophoto Optima 10 on 11 pt by
Keyspools Limited, Golborne, Lancashire, England
Separations by Colorlito, Milano, Italy
Printed and bound in Italy by S A G D O S Spa, Milano
16 15 14 13 12 11 10 9 8 7 6 5 4 3 2 1

Contents

Acknowledgements

The Editor wishes to thank all architects,
designers and manufacturers who supplied
illustrations for reproduction

Introduction

'Themes in Nature' as a heading, would seem to be more appropriate to a chapter on painting, or even music perhaps, rather than to a series of architectural projects; unless these were related to landscape gardening. But although natural settings appear frequently, gardens as such are not prominent in the collection of eighteen interiors that has been assembled for this 68th volume of *Decorative Art*.

The idea came during the first visit to the *Temppeliaukio Church* in Helsinki, by Timo and Tuomo Suomalainen. A church which is also used for concerts, and where on the occasion of that particular visit an orchestral rehearsal was just due to begin. Under the spell of that extraordinary space, one yearned for music that would make the entire church resonate in celebration of some primeval, barbaric ritual. One wished that Stravinsky's *Rite of Spring* could be performed there once a year, to mark the end of winter.

The initial idea, to describe and illustrate an architecture that is expressed with elements of nature, developed, as research progressed, to include also an architecture that responds to the natural environment and, finally, an architecture inspired by a very personal concept of nature. To the first group belongs the *Museum of Contemporary Art in Tehran*, where orientation to the north-east is essential in order to benefit from a purer light. The architects, Kamran Diba and Nader Ardlan, inspired by the traditional wind towers of the local architecture, designed a modular shape that provides reflected light for the underground exhibition galleries. In the *Azuma Residence* by Tadao Ando, the central courtyard that links the two sections of the house is open to sun, wind and rain. In a contrasting mood, preserved skeletons of exotic trees ornate the flat converted by Daniele Boatti in the centre of Milan, Italy.

Numerous projects reflect a concern for the conservation of the environment. Two dune houses, one by William Morgan, in Florida, the other by Claus Bonderup, on a remote coast in the Jutland peninsula, are outstanding examples of underground domestic architecture built in totally opposite climatic conditions. The exciting shape of Antoine Predock's *Solar House*, in New Mexico, shows the many resources of good design within the constraints of a brief that is still subject to much experimentation.

The natural rockface is incorporated into the extension to an old house in the island of Pantelleria, Italy, by the Spanish Studio P.E.R. The new extension includes large open spaces, screened from the fierce mediterranean sun by cane matting resting on concrete columns. Seen from a distance, particularly from the sea, these columns evoke ruins of ancient temples among the vineyards. Another important example of environmental architecture is the *International Museum of Horology* at Chaux-de-Fonds, Switzerland, by Pierre Zoelly and Georges-Jacques Haefely. Partly constructed beneath a well-established city park, the above-ground structures of the museum possess a nobility of line and a monumental quality that merge naturally into the landscape.

The *Hopkins House* in London, and the *Helmuth Schulitz House* near Los Angeles are similar in approach, although the first is a city dwelling built in a protected area of early 19th century Hampstead and the second is perched on a slope in the open countryside. Both architects attempted to replace traditional building methods, involving the employment of costly skilled labour on site, with a system that uses readily available industrial components; in both cases, success depends on the integration of the interiors and the external views, made possible by large expanses of glass. Glass is also used on the hexagonal galleries of the *Vasarely Foundation* at Aix-en-Provence, a building that bears the unmistakable imprint of the artist in the geometry of its plan that still acquires an uncannily organic aspect within the open setting.

The third group of buildings that appear to express a particular idea of nature are mostly holiday homes, with one exception: the *Ingot Coffee Bar* in Kitakyushu, by Shoei Yoh, During day time, the external appearance of the building is that of a mirror to nature, denying the outsider the merest glimpse beyond its enigmatic, reflective facade. Once inside, however, the visitor is surrounded by the image of trees and sky, seen through the one-way mirror walls. The reverse happens as darkness prevails and the brilliantly lit interior is revealed to the passer-by.

The *Hot Dog House* in Illinois, by Stanley Tigerman, is a poetic fantasy that can be inhabited and experienced over and over again. The *House in the Pinewood* at Roccamare, Italy, by Bicocchi and Monsani, is a structure of almost protean quality that, according to the necessity or the whim of the occupants, can be extended into different patterns by enclosing part of the woods, which thus become indoor living spaces. Finally, the *'K' Villa* on Lake Yamanaka, by Shigeru Uchida, is the embodiment of the joy of fulfilment that accompanies the moment of artistic creation. Note its lower level, so firmly rooted into the earth that it appears to be growing out of it; the loveliness of the two wings lightly poised over the square plan; the shape of the sky over the unique central space made for contemplation and quiet happiness.

The advantages offered by plate glass may lead to abuse and loss of control over the essential qualities of a building. In particular, they may threaten an element of architecture that mediates between the interior and the exterior of a building: the window. This is one of the themes developed by Patrick Reyntiens in his article 'Elements of Architecture: The Window'. The author quotes numerous examples from the past to illustrate his thesis, and analyses the success, or lack thereof, in achieving the delicate balance between interior and exterior in modern buildings.

With regard to furninshing, the situation noticed in 1978 appears unchanged. Over the last twelve months, trade fairs have been generally disappointing through lack of new ideas – this is true even of Scandinavia. Industry looks to the past in an attempt to bridge the gap, and certain firms – Cassina of Italy being the most purposeful and serious – are extending their furniture range with replicas of yet more design classics from the 1920's and 1930's. This is quite logical as far as period functional furniture is concerned – after all, that is the purpose of industrial design – but one begins to cringe at the idea of Mackintosh's original pieces, designed for a particular type of interior, being considered as prototypes to be reproduced on an industrial scale, however limited and selective the potential market may be.

The alternative to the widespread lack of initiative on the part of industry rests once more in the hands of individual craftsmen and designers working in isolation or in small groups, and selling direct to the public at prices that compete very favourably with those of high quality industrial production. Sometimes these people started a career in industry, and are therefore able to broaden the scope and the techniques of their individual work with the mechanical skills which a pure craftsman would ignore, and might perhaps despise. The work by Stephen Hogbin, of Canada, proves this point admirably.

In view of such a general development, the last section of the book has been planned in a slightly different way from the past editions of the annual. In an attempt to bring into evidence the link between function and quality of design, measured drawings have been used to illustrate the finer technical points of select items of industrial design. In contrast to this approach, unique pieces by craftsmen and designers have been illustrated in groups, so as to show the phases of development in the style of their makers. It is hoped that these changes will prove useful.

Maria Schofield

Einleitung

Die Übeschrift: "Themen in der Natur" scheint eher zu einem Kapitel über Malerei oder vielleicht sogar Musik als zu einer Reihe architektonischer Projekte zu passen; es sei denn, diese stünden in Beziehung zur Landschaftsgärtnerei. Aber obwohl der natürliche Hintergrund häufig in Erscheinung tritt, nimmt der Garten als solcher in der Auswahl von achtzehn Innenräumen, die für diesen 68. Band der Reihe *Decorative Art* getroffen wurde, keine Sonderstellung ein.

Man kam auf die Idee anläßlich eines ersten Besuches der *Temppeliaukio-Kirche* von Timo und Tuomo Suomalainen in Helsinki. Die Kirche wird auch für Konzertveranstaltungen benutzt, und bei jenem Besuch sollte gerade eine Orchesterprobe beginnen. Ganz unter dem Zauber des ungewöhnlichen Raumes stehend sehnte man sich geradezu nach Musik, die die ganze Kirche zur Feier irgendeines barbarischen Rituals aus der Urzeit widerhallen lassen würde. Man verspürte den Wunsch, dort einmal im Jahr Strawinskys *Sacre du Printemps* zu hören, um so das Ende des Winters zu feiern.

Der ursprüngliche Einfall, eine Architektur zu beschreiben und zu veranschaulichen, die Elemente der Natur als Ausdrucksform verwendet, wurde im Laufe der Studien dazu weiterentwickelt. Man beschloß, eine Architektur in den Themenkreis einzubeziehen, die sich in die natürliche Umgebung einfügt, und schließlich eine Architektur, die von einer äußerst eigenwilligen Naturauffassung inspiriert wird. Zur ersten Gruppe gehört das *Museum für zeitgenössische Kunst in Teheran*, bei dem die Ausrichtung nach Nordosten entscheidend war, wollte man von den besseren Lichtverhältnissen profitieren. Die Architekten, Kamran Diba und Nader Ardlan, ließen sich von den traditionellen Windtürmen der örtlichen Baukunst inspirieren und entwarfen eine modulare Struktur, die die unterirdischen Ausstellungshallen durch Reflektion mit Licht versorgt. Bei der *Azuma-Residenz* von Tadao Ando ist der zentrale Hof, der die beiden Abschnitte des Hauses verbindet, vor Sonne, Wind und Regen ungeschützt. Im Gegensatz dazu schmücken die konservierten Skelette exotischer Bäume die von Daniele Boatti im Zentrum von Milan umgebaute Wohnung.

In zahlreichen Projekten spiegelt sich die Sorge um die Erhaltung der Umwelt wider. Zu den hervorragenden Beispielen unterirdischer Wohnbauten in völlig entgegengesetzten klimatischen Verhältnissen gehören zwei Dünenhäuser, das eine in Florida, von William Morgan, das andere an einem entlegenen Küstenstreifen der Halbinsel Jütland, von Claus Bonderup. Die aufregende Baugestalt des *Solarhauses* von Antoine Predock in Neumexiko zeigt den Einfallsreichtum guten Desings im Rahmen der beschränkten Möglichkeiten einer Bauaufgabe, an deren Verwirklichung man noch immer viel herumexperimentiert.

In den von der spanischen Architekten-gemeinschaft PER auf der Insel Pantelleria in Italien errichteten Anbau an ein altes Haus hat man die natürliche Felswand einbezogen. Zu dem neuen Ergänzungsbau gehören große Freiräume, die durch ein auf Zementsäulen ruhendes Rohrgeflecht gegen die brennende südliche Sonne geschützt sind. Aus der Ferne und besonders vom Meer aus gesehen lassen diese Säulen inmitten der Weinberge Erinnerungen an die Ruinen antiker Tempel aufkommen. Ein weiteres Beispiel für die umweltbezogene Architektur ist das *Internationale Uhrmacherkunstmuseum* von Pierrre Zoelly und Georges-Jacques Haefely in Chaux-de-Fonds in der Schweiz. Die überirdischen Strukturen des zum Teil unter dem gepflegten alten Stadtpark angelegten Museums zeichnen sich durch die Erhabenheit der Linie und durch eine gewisse Großartigkeit aus, die sich ganz natürlich in der Landschaft fortsetzen.

Von gleichem Geist durchdrungen sind das *Hopkins-Haus* in London und das *Helmuth-Schulitz-Haus* in der Nähe von Los Angeles, obwohl es sich bei dem ersten um ein städtisches Wohnhaus in einem Konservierungsviertel Hampsteads aus dem frühen neunzehnten Jahrhundert handelt, während sich das zweite auf einem Abhang in offener Landschaft befindet. Beide Architekten versuchten, die traditionellen Bauverfahren, welche die Beschäftigung kostspieliger Fachkräfte auf der Baustelle mit sich bringen, durch ein Konstruktionssystem mit leicht zu beschaffenden vorgefertigten Einzelteilen zu ersetzen. In beiden Fällen beruht der Erfolg des Gebäudes auf die Integration von Innenraum und Aussicht, die durch riesige Glasflächen ermöglicht wird. Auch bei den sechseckigen Ausstellungsräumen der *Vasarely-Stiftung* in Aix-en-Provence spielt Glas eine Rolle. In der Geometrie seines Grundrisses, dem die offene

Landschaft einen unheimlich organischen Aspekt verleiht, trägt das Gebäude unverkennbar den Stempel des Künstlers.

Bei der dritten Gruppe von Bauten, die einer besonderen Naturauffassung Ausdruck zu verleihen scheinen, handelt es sich meistens um Ferienhäuser, mit einer Ausnahme: die *Ingot Coffee-Bar* von Shoei Yoh in Kitakyushu. Am Tage stellt das Äußere des Gebäudes einen Spiegel der Natur dar, der dem Draußenstehenden kienen Blick hinter die rätselhafte, die Umwelt reflektierende Fassade gestattet. Im Innern jedoch ist der Besucher vom Bild der Bäume und des Himmels, das er durch die nur den Ausblick gestattenden Spiegelwände sieht, umgeben. Das Gegenteil geschieht in der Dunkelheit, und dem Vorübergehenden offenbart sich der hellerleuchtete Innenraum.

Das *Hot-Dog-Haus* von Stanley Tigerman in Illinois ist ein poetisches Phantasiegebilde, das man bewohnen und immer wieder von neuem erleben kann. Das *Haus im Pinienwald* von Bicocchi und Monsani ist eine Struktur von nahezu proteischem Charakter, das sich je nach den Bedürfnissen oder der Laune seiner Bewohner erweitern und in seiner Anlage verändern läßt, indem man einen Teil der Wälder einbezieht und diese damit zu bewohnbaren Innenräumen macht. Zum Abschluss die *'K'-Villa* von Shigeru Uchida, die die Fruede am Gefühl des Erfülltseins verkörpert, von dem der künstlerische Schöpfungsakt begleitet wird. Man beachte den unteren Teil des Hauses, der so fest in der Erde verwurzelt ist, daß er aus ihr hervorzuwachsen scheint; die Schönheit der beiden Flügel, die sich schwerelos über dem viereckigen Grundriß erheben; der Ausblick auf den Himmel von dem einmaligen Freiraum in der Mitte, der für den Zustand der Besinnlichkeit und des stillen Glücks wie geschaffen scheint.

Die Vorteile, die such aus der Verwendung von Tafelglas ergeben, können leicht zu Mißbrauch und Verlust an Kontrolle über die wesentlichen Merkmale eines Gebäudes führen. Insbesondere können sie jenes Element der Architektur bedrohen, das zwischen dem Innenraum und der Außenform eines Baus vermittelt: das Fenster. Dies ist eines der Themen, die Patrick Reyntiens in seinem Artikel: "Elemente der Architektur: das Fenster" erörtert. Zur Veranschaulichung seiner These führt der Verfasser zahlreiche Beispiele aus der Vergangenheit an, und er analysiert die Gründe für den Erfolg oder Missßerfolg bei dem Bestreben, die nur allzu leicht gestörte Harmonie

zwischen dem Inneren und Außeren moderner Gebäude zu verwirklichen.

In bezug auf die Möbelherstellung scheint sich die Lage seit 1978 nicht verändert zu haben. Während der letzten zwölf Monate waren die Fachmessen aufgrund des Ideenmangels allgemein enttäuschend – das gilt sogar für Skandinavien. Bei dem Versuch, diese Lücke zu schließen, greift die Industrie auf die Vergangenheit zurück, und bestimmte Firmen – unter denen die italienische Firma Cassina besonders dynamisch und ernstzunehmen ist – erweitern ihr Möbelangebot mit ständig neuen Nachahmungen der klassischen Designerfolge der zwanziger und dreißiger Jahre. Soweit es sich um funktionale Stilmöbel handelt, ist dies durchaus logisch – schließlich liegt darin der Zweck industriellen Designs –, jedoch ist einem der Gedanke peinlich, daß ein Originalstück von Mackintosh, welches seinerzeit für einen bestimmten Typ von Innenausstattung entworfen wurde, jetzt erneut als Prototyp für die industrielle Fertigung in Frage kommen soll – so begrenzt und exklusiv der potentielle Absatzmarkt auch sein mag.

Die Alternative zu dem allgemeinen Mangel an Initiative auf seiten der Industrie liegt wieder einmal in Händen individueller Kunsthand-werker und Designer, die allein oder in kleinen Gruppen arbeiten und direkt an die Öffentlichkeit verkaufen, zu Preisen, die bei einem Vergleich mit denen der hochgütigen Industrieerzeugung äußerst günstig abschneiden.

Angesichts einer derartigen allgemeinen Entwicklung hat man den letzten Teil des vorliegenden Buches etwas abweichend von früheren Ausgaben der Serie gestaltet. In dem Bestreben, den engen Zusammenhang zwischen Funktion und Güte beim Design aufzuzeigen, hat man maßstäbliche Zeichnungen verwandt, um feinere technische Einzelheiten der ausgewählten Beispiele industriellen Designs zu veranschaulichen. Im Gegensatz dazu hat man einmalige Arbeiten von Kunsthandwerkern und Designern in Gruppen zusammengefaßt illustriert. Damit will man die einzelnen Entwicklungsphasen im Stil der Hersteller aufzeigen. Wir hoffen, daß sich diese Änderungen als nützlich erweisen werden.

Maria Schofield

Introducción

'Temas en la naturaleza' como título parecería ser mas apropiado para un capítulo sobre pintura, o tal vez incluso sobre música, que para una serie de proyectos de arquitectura, a menos que estos estuviesen relacionados can paisajismo de jardines. Pero aunque los escenarios naturales aparecen con frecuencia, los jardines propiamente dichos no destacan en la colección de dieciocho interiores recopilados para este volumen 68 de *Decorative Art*.

La idea se originó durante la primera visita realizada a la *Iglesia de Temppeliaukio* en Helsinki, obra de Timo y Tuomo Suomalainen. Este templo tambien se usa para conciertos y en dicha ocasión estaba a punto de comenzar un ensayo orquestal. Bajo el encanto de aquel extraordinario espacio, uno sentia ansia de música que hiciese resonar toda la iglesia en celebración de un ritual primitivo y barbárico. Uno sentía el deseo de que 'La Consagración de la Primavera' de Stravinsky pudiera interpretarse allí una vez al año para señalar el final del invierno.

La idea inicial de describir e ilustrar una arquitectura que se expresa con elementos de la naturaleza se desarrolló, a medida que fue progresando la investigación, para incluir también una arquitecturea que responde al ambiente natural y, finalmente, una arquitectura inspirada por un concepto de naturaleza muy personal. Al primer grupo pertenece el *Museo de Arte Contemporáneo de Teherán*, donde la orientación hacia el noreste es esencial con el fin de beneficiarse de una luz más pura. Los arquitectos Kamran Diba y Nader Ardlan, inspirados por las tradicionales torres de viento de la arquitectura local, diseñaron una forma modular que proporciona luz reflejada para las galerías de exposición subterráneas. En la *Residencia Azuma* de Tadao Ando, el patio central que comunica a las dos secciones de la casa está abierto al sol, viento y lluvia. En una disposición de contraste los esqueletos preservados de árboles exóticos adornan el apartamento convertido por Daniele Boatti en el centro de Milán, Italia.

Un gran número de proyectos reflejan preocupación por la conservación del medio ambiente. Dos casas de dunas, una de ellas obra de William Morgan en la Florida y la otra de Claus Bonderup en una costa remota de la península de Jutlandia, constituyen ejemplos excepcionales de la arquitecura doméstica subterránea construida en condiciones climatológicas totalmente opuestas. La forma interesantísima de la *Casa Solar* de Antoine Predock en Nuevo México muestra los diversos recursos de buen diseño dentro de las limitaciones de un detalle que todavía es objeto de mucha experimentación.

La roca natural se ve incorporoda en la extensión de una vieja casa en la isla de Pantelleria, Italia, por parte del estudio español PER. La nueva extensión incluye grandes espacios abiertos protegidos del intenso sol mediterráneo mediante esteras de caña sobre columnas de hormigón. Vistas a distancia, especialmente desde el mar, estas columnas evocan ruinas de templos antiguos entre los viñedos. Otro ejemplo importante de arquitectura ambiental es el *Museo Internacional de Horología* en Chaux-de-Fonds, Suiza, obra de Pierre Zoelly y Georges-Jacques Haefely. Construido parcialmente bajo un parque bien establecido, las estructuras del museo sobre el suelo poseen una nobleza de línea y una calidad monumental que se unen naturalmente con el paisaje.

La *Casa Hopkins* en Londres y la *Casa Helmuth Schulitz* cerca de Los Angeles ofrecen un enfoque similar, si bien la primera es una vivienda de ciudad construida en una zona protegida de arquitectura de principios del siglo XIX en Hampstead y la segunda está asentada en un declive en campo abierto. Los arquitectos de ambas edificaciones intentaron sustituir los métodos tradicionales de construcción, incluyendo el empleo de costosa mano de obra especializada, por un sistema que utiliza componentes industriales fácilmente disponibles. En ambos casos, el éxito depende de la integración de los interiores y de las vistas exteriores, todo lo cual es posible mediante grandes extensiones de cristalería. También se usa vidrio en las galerías hexagonales de la *Fundación Vasarely* en Aix-en-Provence, un edificio que posee el inconfundible distintivo del artista en la geometría de su planta y que todavía adquiere un aspecto extraordinariamente orgánico dentro del marco abierto.

El tercer grupo de edificios que parecen expresar una idea particular de la naturaleza son mayormente casas veraniegas, con una excepción: el *Café Ingot* en Kitakyushu obra de Shoei Yoh. Durante el día, la apariencia externa del edificio es como un espejo de la naturaleza, negándole al forastero el mínimo vislumbre más allá de su fachada enigmática y reflectante. No obstante, una vez en su interior, uno se ve rodeado por la imagen de árboles y firmamento, vistos a través de las paredes de espejos unidireccionales. Lo contrario ocurre a medida que prevalece la oscuridad y el interior brillantemente iluminado se revela al transeúnte.

La *Casa Hot Dog* en Illinois, obra de Stanley Tigerman, es una fantasía poética que se puede habitar y experimentar una y otra vez. La *Casa en el Pinar* situada en Roccamare, Italia, obra de Bicocchi y Monsani, es una estructura de calidad casi proteica la cual, según la necesidad o antojo de los ocupantes, puede extenderse en formas diferentes encerrando parte del pinar para convertirlo así en viviendas interiores. Por último, la *Villa 'K'* sobre el Lagos Yamanaka, obra de Shigeru Uchida, es la personificación de la alegría de satisfacción que acompaña el momento de la creación artística. Observe su planta inferior, tan firmemente enterrada que parece brotar de la misma tierra, la belleza de las dos alas ligeramente equilibradas sobre la planta cuadrada, la forma del firmamento sobre ese exclusivo espacio central hecho para contemplación y tranquilidad.

Las ventajas que ofrece el vidrio cilindrado pueden conducir al abuso y pérdida de control sobre las características esenciales de un edificio. En particular, pueden amenazar un elemento de arquitectura que media entre el interior y el exterior de un edificio: la ventana. Este es uno de los temas desarrollados por Patrick Reyntiens en su artículo titulado 'Elementos de arquitectura: la ventana'. El autor cita numerosos ejamplos del pasado para ilustrar su tesis y analiza el éxito, o fracaso, en conseguir el equilibrio delicado entre el interior y el exterior en los edificios modernos.

En lo que respecta al mobiliario, la situación observada en 1978 parece inalterada. Durante los últimos doce meses, las ferias de muestras han decepcionado generalmente por falta de nuevas ideas, lo cual puede decirse incluso de los países escandinavos. La industria mira al pasado en un intento de llenar ese vacío y algunas empresas, tales como Cassina de Italia que es la más determinada y seria, están ampliando su serie de muebles con réplicas de aún más clásicos del diseño de los años 20 y 30. Esto es muy lógico en lo que respecta a muebles

functionales de época – después de todo, esa es la finalidad del diseño industrial – pero uno empieza a encogerse ante la idea de considerar las piezas originales de Mackintosh, diseñadas para un tipo de interior determinado, como prototipos de reproducción a escala industrial, por muy limitado y selectivo que pueda ser el potencial del mercado.

La alternativa a la falta de iniciativa muy difundida por parte de la industria reposa una vez más en las manos de los artesanos y diseñadores individuales que trabajan aisladamente o en pequeños grupos y venden directamente al público a precios que son muy competitivos con aquellos de la producción industrial de alta calidad. A veces sucede que estas personas iniciaron una carrera en la industria y, por consiguiente, tienen capacidad para ampliar el ámbito y las técnicas de su trabajo individual con los medios mecánicos que un verdadero artesano no usaría y quizás llegase a despreciar. Este punto lo demuestra admirablemente el trabajo del canadiense Stephen Hogbin.

En vista de un desarrollo tan general, la última sección del libro fue planeada de manera un poco diferente a las pasadas ediciones del anuario. En un intento de poner en evidencia la relación entre la función y la calidad de diseño se han utilizado dibujos dimensionados para ilustrar los puntos técnicos más finos de artículos selectos de diseño industrial. En contraste con este enfoque, los ejemplares exclusivos de artesanos y diseñadores se han ilustrado en grupos con objeto de mostrar las fases de desarrollo en el estilo de sus creadores. Esperamos que estos cambios resulten útiles.

María Schofield

Introduction

Le titre de 'Thèmes dans la Nature' semblerait mieux convenir à un chapitre sur la peinture, ou même peut-être sur la musique, qu'à une série de projets architecturaux, à moins que ceux-ci concernent les jardins paysagers. Mais bien que les sites naturels apparaissent fréquemment, les jardins en tant que tels ne sont pas prépondérants dans la collection de dix-huit intérieurs qui a été assemblée pour ce 68ème volume de *Decorative Art*.

L'idée est née lors d'une première visite à *l'Eglise Temppeliaukio* d'Helsinki, réalisée par Timo et Tuomo Suomalainen. Cette église est aussi utilisée pour des concerts et lors de cette visite un orchestre se préparait à répéter. Sous le charme de ce lieu extraordinaire, on se prend à désirer ardemment une musique qui ferait résonner l'église tout entière dans la célébration de rites primitifs et barbares. On en vient à souhaiter que le *Sacre du Printemps* de Stravinski puisse être exécuté ici une fois par an, pour marquer la fin de l'hiver.

L'idée initiale, la description et l'illustration d'une architecture qui s'exprime par des éléments de la nature, s'est peu à peu développée au fur et à mesure de la recherche pour englober une architecture qui réagit à l'environnement naturel et finalement, une architecture qui s'inspire d'une conception très personnelle de la nature. Le *Musée d'Art Contemporain de Téhéran*, dont l'orientation au nord-est est essentielle afin de bénéficier d'une lumière plus pure, appartient au premier groupe. Les architectes, Kamran Diba et Nader Ardlan, s'inspirant des tours à vent traditionnelles de l'architecture locale, ont conçu une forme modulaire qui réfléchit la lumière pour les galeries d'exposition souterraines. Dans la *Résidence Azuma* de Tadao Ando la cour centrale qui relie les deux sections de la maison est ouverte au soleil, au vent et à la pluie. Par contraste, les squelettes conservés d'arbres exotiques ornent l'appartement transformé par Daniele Boatti au centre de Milan, en Italie.

De nombreux projets reflètent le souci de la conservation de l'environnement. Deux maisons des dunes, l'une créée par William Morgan en Floride et l'autre par Claus Bonderup sur une côte isolée de la péninsule du Jutland, sont des exemples remarquables d'architecture domestique souterraine dans des conditions climatiques complètement opposées. La forme impressionnante de la *Maison Solaire* d'Antoine Predock au Nouveau-Mexique est une indication des nombreuses ressources d'une bonne architecture en dépit des limites d'un concept qui fait toujours l'objet de beaucoup d'expérimentation.

Dans l'île de Pantelleria, en Italie, le Studio espagnol PER a incorporé la surface rocheuse dans le cadre de l'agrandissement d'une vieille maison. Les nouveaux bâtiments comprennent de grands espaces ouverts, protégés du féroce soleil méditerranéen par des auvents de bambou reposant sur des colonnes en béton. Vues de loin, et surtout de la mer, ces colonnes évoquent les ruines de temples anciens parmi les vignes. Un autre exemple important d'architecture incorporée à l'environnement est le *Musée international d'Horlogerie* de Chaux-de-Fonds, en Suisse, créé par Pierre Zoelly et Georges-Jacques Haefely. Le musée est construit en partie au-dessous d'un parc public très fréquenté et les structures visibles possèdent une noblesse de ligne et une qualité monumentale qui se confondent naturellement avec le paysage.

La *Maison Hopkins* de Londres et la *Maison Helmuth Schulitz* près de Los Angeles révèlent une approche similaire, bien que la première soit un bâtiment citadin construit dans une zone protégée de Hampstead datant du début du 19ème siècle et que la deuxième soit perchée sur une pente en pleine compagne. Les deux architectes ont essayé de remplacer des méthodes de construction traditionnelles nécessitant l'emploi sur place d'une main-d'oeuvre qualifiée et coûteuse par un système permettant d'utiliser des éléments industriels facilement disponibles; dans les deux cas, le succès repose sur l'intégration des intérieurs et des vues extérieures, rendue possible par de grandes surfaces vitrées. Le verre a aussi été utilisé sur les galeries hexagonales de la *Fondation Vasarely* d'Aix-en-Provence, un bâtiment qui porte le chachet indéniable de l'artiste dans la géométrie du plan et qui revêt pourtant un aspect étrangement organique dans le site ouvert.

Le troisième groupe de bâtiments, qui semblent exprimer une conception particulière de la nature, sont généralement des maisons de vilégiature, avec une exception : le *Café Ingot de* Kitakyushu, créé par Shoei Yoh. Pendant la journée, l'aspect extérieur du bâtiment est celui d'un miroir reflétant la nature et refusant à celui qui le contemple le plus petit aperçu de ce qui est au-delà de sa façade réfléchissante et énigmatique. Une fois à l'intérieur, le visiteur se trouve toutefois entouré de l'image des arbres et du ciel, vus à travers les murs qui sont des miroirs d'un seul côté. Une fois la nuit tombée, l'inverse se produit et l'intérieur est révélé aux passants, brillamment éclairé.

La *Hot Dog House* de Stanley Tigerman, dans l'Illinois, est une vision poétique où l'on peut habiter et dont on peut faire l'expérience autant de fois qu'on le veut. La *Maison dans la Pinède* de Bicocchi et Monsani à Roccamare, en Italie, est une structure de caractère presque protéen qui selon les besoins ou la fantaisie de ses occupants peut être agrandie de diverses façons en englobant une partie des bois, qui deviennent ainsi des espaces vivants intégrés à l'intérieur. Enfin, la *Villa 'K'* du lac Yamanaka, par Shigeru Uchida, est l'incarnation même de la joie et de la plénitude qui accompagnent l'instant de la création artistique. On remarquera le niveau inférieur, si fermement enraciné dans le sol qu'il semble en être sorti, l'aspect charmant des deux ailes qui reposent en èquilibre sur le plan carré et la forme du ciel au-dessus de l'espace central unique en son genre et consacré à la contemplation et à la sérénité.

Les avantages offerts par le verre à glaces peuvent entraîner des excès et une perte de contrôle sur les qualités essentielles d'un bâtiment. Ils risquent plus particulièrement de menacer un élément de l'architecture qui sert de médiateur entre l'intérieur et l'extérieur d'un bâtiment : la fenêtre. Ceci est l'un des thèmes traités par Patrick Reyntiens dans son article 'Eléments d'Architecture : La Fenêtre'. L'auteur cite de nombreux exemples du passé pour illustrer sa thèse et il analyse comment l'équilibre délicat qui existe entre l'intérieur et l'extérieur des bâtiments modernes a été ou non réalisé.

En ce qui concerne l'ameublement, la situation telle qu'elle apparaissait en 1978 ne semble pas avoir changé. Au cours des douze derniers mois, les foires commerciales ont été généralement décevantes par leur manque d'idées nouvelles, et ceci est même vrai pour la Scandinavie. L'industrie se tourne verse le passé pour combler cette lacune et certaines firmes (celle de Cassina en Italie étant la plus réfléchie et la plus sérieuse) agrandissent leur gamme de meubles grâce à des répliques, encore et toujours, des classiques des années 20 et 30. Ceci est tout à fait logique en ce qui concerne l'ameublement fonctionnel de style (c'est après tout l'objet de l'esthétique industrielle) mais l'on commence à s'inquiéter à l'idée que des pièces originales de Mackintosh, conçues pour un type particulier d'intérieur, puissent être considérées comme des prototypes pouvant être reproduits à une échelle industrielle, tant limité et sélectif que soit le marché potentiel.

Devant ce manque d'initiative généralisé de la part de l'industrie, l'avenir semble être entre les mains une fois de plus d'artisans et de créateurs travaillant seuls ou en petits groupes et vendant directement au public à des prix qui font concurrence très favorablement à ceux de la production industrielle de qualité supérieure. Ces individus ont parfois commencé leur carrière dans l'industrie et sont donc en mesure d'élargir le champ et les techniques de leur travail individuel grâce aux ressources mécaniques qu'un pur artisan ne connaîtrait pas et pourrait même mépriser. Le travail de Stephen Hogbin au Canada en est une preuve admirable.

Etant donné le caractère de ce développement général, la dernière section du livre a été organisée différemment que dans les éditions précédentes de cette publication annuelle. Afin de mettre en évidence le lien qui existe entre la fonction et la qualité du design nous avons utilisé des dessins accompagnés de mesures pour illustrer les points techniques subtils de certains articles sélectionnés de l'esthétique industrielle. Par contraste, nous avons illustré en groupes des pièces uniques réalisées par des artisans et des créateurs afin d'indiquer les phases de développement du style des fabricants. Nous espérons que ces modifications s'avéreront utiles.

Maria Schofield

序　章

「自然をテーマに」という表題は、建築作品が造園に関係していない場合には、一連の建築作品に対してより、むしろ絵画とか音楽とかのほうにふさわしいように思える。この「装飾の芸術」第68巻に収録されている18のインテリアの中には、自然を背景にしたものがかなりあるが、この表題にふさわしい庭園はそれほど多くはない。

この表題を思いついたのは、ヘルシンキにある、ティモとトゥオモというスオマライネン兄弟の作品「テンッペリアウキオ教会」をはじめて訪れたときである。この教会は、コンサートにも利用され、私が訪れたときには、ちょうどオーケストラのリハーサルが、始まろうとしていた。この、ものすごく広大な空間に立つと、ある古代の、荒々しい儀式のときに奏でられる、教会全体をゆるがすような音楽を聞きたくなった。冬の終りを告げるために、ストラビンスキーの「春の祭典」が、年に一度、ここで演奏されたらどんなにいいだろうと思った。

最初は、自然の要素を表現している建築物を、この巻で説明し、描写しようと思ったが、調査がすすむにつれて、自然環境に呼応する建築物をも含めるようになり、最後には、自然に関する非常に個人的な概念から生まれた建築物も含めることにした。第一のグループに属するものとしては、「テヘラン現代美術館」があげられるが、ここでは、より安定した光を採り入れるため、北東に位置することが重要なことであった。カムラン・ディバとナデル・アルドランの2人の建築家は、この地方に昔から伝わる風の塔にヒントを得、地下の展示室に反射光が入るようなモジュール型を考案した。安藤忠雄の「アズマ・レジデンス」では、中央の中庭が、家の二つの部分を結んでいるが、そこには、太陽や風や雨が入るようになっている。これとは対照的なのが、ダニエル・ボアッティが改修した、ミラノの中心にある住居で、風変りな枯木が装飾に使われている。

周囲の自然保護を考慮に入れた建築物も多々ある。ウイリアム・モーガンは、フロリダに、クラウス・ボンデルップは、ユトランド半島の先端の海岸の砂丘に、家を建てたが、この二軒は、まったく正反対の気象条件に建てられた地下家屋の好例である。ニューメキシコにあるアントワーヌ・

プレドックの「ソーラー・ハウス」のすばらしい形は、まだまだ、多くの実験を必要としてはいるが、簡易建築物の制約の枠内でそこから優秀なデザインが多く生まれ出る可能性がある。

イタリアのパンテレリア島にある古い屋敷の離れは、スペインのスタジオPERが建てたものだが、そこには、自然の岩肌がとり入れられている。その新しい離れには、広大な開けた広間があり、コンクリートの円柱にかかっている木の茎でできたすだれが、強い地中海の日光をさえぎっている。遠くから、特に海の方から見ると、これらの円柱は、ブドウ畑にそびえる古代の寺院の廃墟を思いおこさせる。周囲の自然保護を考慮に入れた建築でもう一つ大切なのは、ピエール・ズェリーとジョルジュ＝ジャック・ヘーファリーによるスイスのショー・ド・フォンにある「国際時計博物館」である。この一部は、すばらしい市立公園の地下に建てられているが、地上の部分は、気品のある線と記念碑的趣きを持ち、周囲の景色にうまく融合している。

ロンドンの「ホプキンズ邸」とロサンゼルス近郊の「ヘルムート・シュリッツ邸」とは、似たようなアプローチで建てられたのであるが、前者は、19世紀初頭のハムプステッド保護地区に建てられた都市住宅であり、後者は、広々としたいなかの斜面に建てられたものである。両建築家は共に、高賃金の熟練工を現場で働かせるということも含めた、従来の建築方法を、容易に手に入れることのできる工場で作られた部品を用いる方法に代えようとしたのである。どちらの場合にも、成功は、屋外の景色とインテリアとの統合にかかっていたのであるが、これは、ガラスの大幅な利用によって達成されたのである。ガラスは、エクサン・プロバンスにある「バザルリー基金」の六角形の画廊にも用いられているが、この建物は、そのオープン・セッティングの枠内で、不思議と系統立った面を持っており、まぎれもないこの建築家のおもかげを残している。

自然に関する特別な概念を表現しているように思われる第三のグループは、殆どが休日用の家屋であるが、ただ一つの例外は、福岡にある葉祥栄の「インゴット・コーヒー・バー」である。昼の間は、この建物の外観は、自然を写す鏡のようであり、外からでは、その不思議な反射する正面を通して、中を一瞥することすらできない。しかし、いったん中に入ると、一方からしか見えない鏡の壁を通して見える木々や空に囲まれてしまう。日が暮れて暗闇になると、これとは反対の現象が起こり、明かるく照明された内部が、道行く人々に照らし出されるのである。

イリノイ州にあるスタンリー・タイガーマンの「ホット・ドッグ・ハウス」は、何回でもそこに住んで、経験できる詩的なファンタジーである。イタリアのロカモアにあるビュッキとモンサーニの「松林の家」は、変幻自在な構造であり、住む人の必要や気分に応じて、林の一部分を囲みこんで、屋内の居住スペースとし、異ったパターンに拡張できるのである。最後に、山中湖にある内田繁の「Kヴィラ」は、芸術的創造の瞬間に体験する、何かを成しとげたという喜びを具現している。その下の方に注意してみると、あまりにしっかりと地面に根をおろしているので、まるでそこから生えてきたように見える。二つの棟は、四角い敷地にうまい具合いに釣合いをとって建っている。そのユニークな中央のスペースの上の空の形は、黙考と静かな幸せを表わしている。

板ガラスのもたらすさまざまな利点は、濫用され、建物の必須的特性をコントロールできなくなる可能性がある。特に、建物の内部と外部の間に介在する建築要素である窓をおびやかす可能性がある。この事は、パトリック・レインティエンが、「建築の要素——窓」の中で提起しているテーマの一つである。彼は、自分の論旨を例証するために、過去の例を数多く引用し、現代建築における内部と外部との微妙なバランスの成功例とそうでない場合とを分析している。

室内装飾に関しては、1978年に述べた状況に変化がないようである。この12か月の間に行われた見本市は、大体において、新鮮なアイディア不足のため、魅力に欠けるものであった これは、スカンジナビアの場合でさえも言えることである。家具業界は、そのギャップを埋めるため、過去に目を向けており、1920年代、1930年代の色々な古典的デザインのレプリカを、家具のレパートリーに加えた会社もあり、特に、イタリアのカッシーナ社は、もっとも意欲的に、まじめにこれに取組んでいる。これは、時代物の機能的家具に関する限りは、まったく論理的なことである 結局、このことこそが、工業デザインの目的なのである しかし、マッキントッシュのオリジナル作品は、その潜在的市場は限定されたものであるかもしれないが、特別な型のインテリアのために設計され、工業的スケールで復製されるべき原型であるとみなされているという考えに、人々は恐れを感じはじめている。

一般に工業側に、欠けているイニシャティブは、個人又は小グループで仕事をし、質の良い工業製品と十分にたちうちできる値段で、作品を直接大衆に販売している工芸家やデザイナーの手の中にあるのである。こうした人々の中には、工場で、最初に仕事を覚え、それゆえに、生粋の工芸家が無視し、軽べつさえするかもしれない機械技術を使って彼ら個々の仕事の範囲や技術を広げ得る人もいるのである。カナダのスティーブン・ホグビンの仕事は、この点を見事に証明している。

このような一般的発展を顧慮して、この本の最後の部分は、これまでの年鑑とは、多少違った趣にしようと思っている。デザインの機能と質との関連性を明らかにするために、寸法入りの図面を用いて、工業デザインの中から精選された作品の詳しい技術上の点を説明し、また、このアプローチとは対照的に、工芸家やデザイナーのユニークな作品を、いくつかのグループにまとめて、それぞれの製作者のスタイルの発展過程を示している。このような今までと違ったとり上げ方が役に立てば幸いである。

マリア・スコフィールド

Themes in Nature

The Museum of Contemporary Art in Tehran, Iran

architects:
D.A.Z. Architects
Planners and Engineers
Design team: Kamran Diba,
Nader Ardlan

photography:
B Zohdi

The plan of this museum has a strong, graphic quality: it consists of a square element firmly wedged into a geometrical shape composed of two larger, interlocking squares. Six main blocks are asymmetrically placed around the edge of the basic shape, so as to face north-east. The rigidity of the square form is then tempered by semicircular accretions that offer the intimacy of secluded exhibition spaces within the large gallery blocks and, projecting into the central open space, contribute to the free form of the sculpture court.

The building is partly underground, on a sunken site at the western edge of Farah Park. When approaching from the north the above-ground structure is completely exposed, but from the southern approach the building is hidden by an artificial hill housing the auxiliary facilities around the main hall.

From the entrance lobby to the exhibition spaces the transition is immediate: a brief passage leads

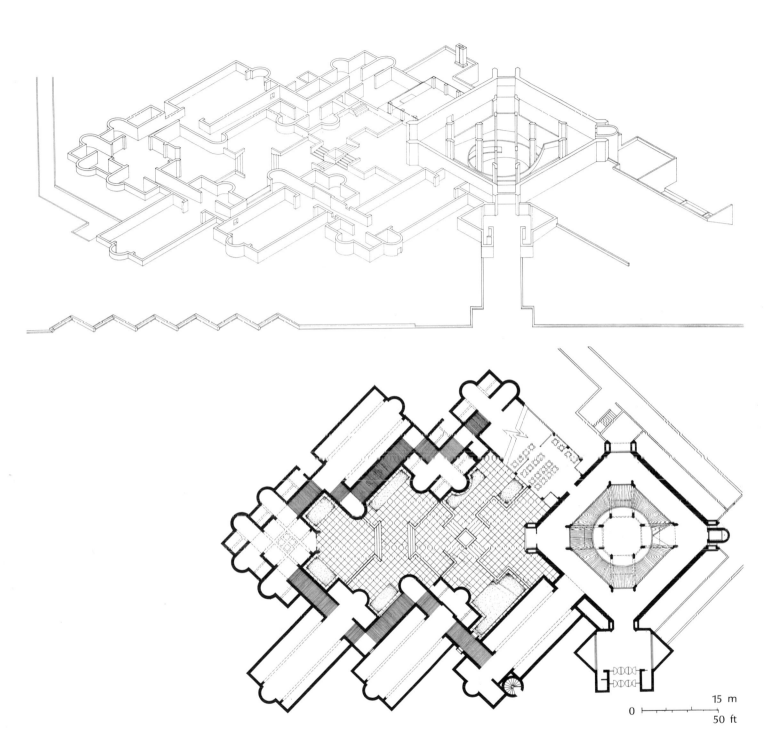

1 Aerial view of the Museum, clearly showing the characteristic fenestration oriented to the north-east

2 Axonometric and plan

15 m

0   50 ft

to Gallery 1, which in turn communicates directly with Gallery 2 and, through glass doors, with the sculpture court. Gallery 1 is at the top level of a vertical element that plunges underground to the lowest gallery level and is the fulcrum of the building. The main circulation pattern begins at Gallery 2 with a system of low-gradient ramps forming a circuit that links the galleries, from the entrance level at Gallery 2 down to Gallery 9, then up again from Gallery 9

to Gallery 1 at main entrance level. This particular treatment recalls the Iranian bazaar which architecturally absorbs people into a sequence of unfolding large and small spaces in a continuous circulation system. A feeling of compulsion, inherent in such a pre-determined itinerary, is relieved by numerous openings in the walls, directed both inside and outside the building, and by connecting Gallery 5 to the central open court.

3 General view; in the background are the four light wells placed at the cardinal points over the main hall

4 Perspective of typical gallery

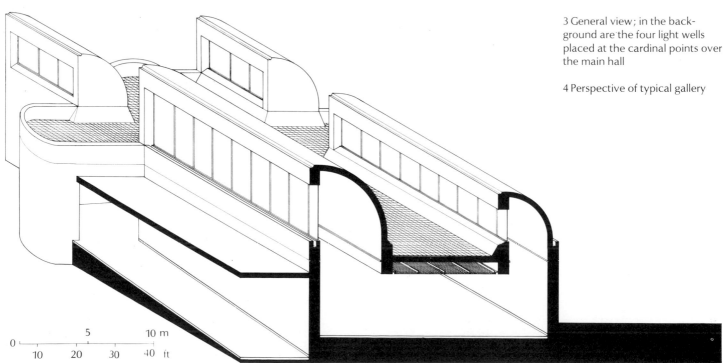

0 5 10 m
10 20 30 40 ft

5 Section of main hall

6 View of main hall showing the
circular ramp linking the different
levels

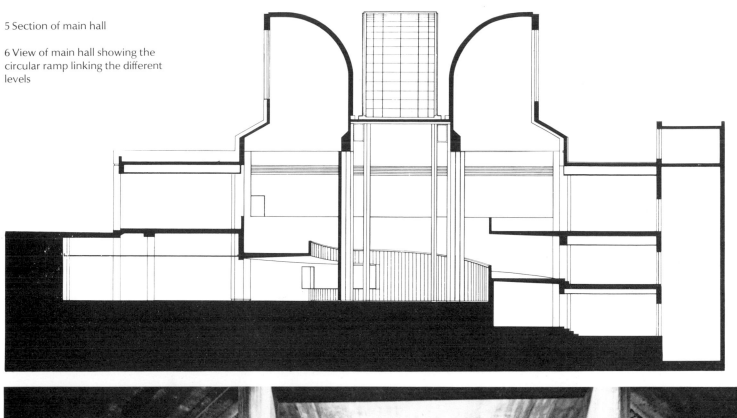

7 Looking upwards to the light wells

8 Fish-eye view from main hall; on foreground is the oil and steel sculpture by Haraguchi with reflections of the windows from the light wells above

The most important effect of this particular system of horizontal planes is the utilization of direct and reflected light coming from the same direction. Inspired by the characteristic ventilation towers of traditional local architecture, the 'baad-geers' (literally: 'wind-catchers') the designers created the architectural shape of the four light wells that are placed over the four corners of the vertical element of the building, symbolically facing the cardinal points. By repeating the basic shape on a smaller scale, and also by developing it into long galleries, the architects obtained a system of staggered fenestration based on a working principle similar to that of the 'baad-geers': the north-east light, 'caught' by means of the window, is directed by the curved shape of the light well inside the gallery, while the south-west light falling on the copper-clad light wells outside is reflected towards the windows. The quality of natural light in the galleries is therefore controlled as far as possible, but artificial lighting

7

9 One of the exhibition galleries; note the position of the windows which guarantees that natural light is reflected by the wall above the low central ceiling

10 View from Gallery 5 across the central court; in the background are the four light towers

supplements and occasionally substitutes natural light sources, as for example in Gallery 9.

The declivity of the central open space is negotiated by a series of varying floor levels, connected by a symmetrical pattern of steps. The roofscape becomes available and accessible at this point, and acquires a visual reference to the vernacular roofscapes of traditional Iranian architecture, translated into a functional and contemporary idiom. As an open air transition

between Gallery 1 and the underground gallery circuit, this space could be aptly described as the lungs of the building. A permanent collection of sculptures is exhibited there, and open air festivals of theatre, dance and music are also held. Construction is in situ concrete on stone walling, complemented by plate and mirror glass. All service ducts are placed above metal tracking on ceilings. Total floor area is 7000m^2 (75,300 ft^2) and exhibition wall space is 2,500m^2 (26,900 ft^2).

The Azuma Residence in Osaka, Japan

architect:
Tadao Ando

photography:
Tadao Ando Architect
and Associates

In an urban context, this house symbolises an isolated unit of the traditional timber row-house called 'nagaya', a comparatively low-cost urban housing form where a series of small dwellings, 3–5m × 15m on average, share common party walls and a continuous communal roof, but have individual entrances normally opening directly onto the street. A very popular form of housing in the past, the nagaya began to decline during the reconstruction period following the second World War and is now rapidly disappearing.

The plan of the old house that stood on the site before re-construction shows a cluster of rooms occupying the front portion of the first level, while an open court is left at the back of the house; on the second level, an open space is enclosed between two symmetrical rooms. In an attempt to express the spirit of the traditional concept in a modern house, architect Tadao Ando decided to emphasize the centrifugal effect of this inner open space, which now cuts through the entire section.

11 Outside view; the house re-
places the central section of a
three-dwellings nagaya, and
occupies a site of 57m² (610 ft.²)

12 Plans of the original house
    1 Entrance
    2 Dining/kitchen
    3 Storage
    4 Tatami
    5 Toilet
    6 Open court

13 Plans and section of present
house
    1 Entrance lobby
    2 Living room
    3 Light court
    4 Dining/kitchen
    5 Bathroom
    6 Master bedroom
    7 Suspended deck
    8 Study bedroom

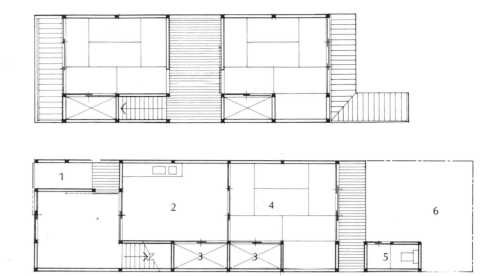

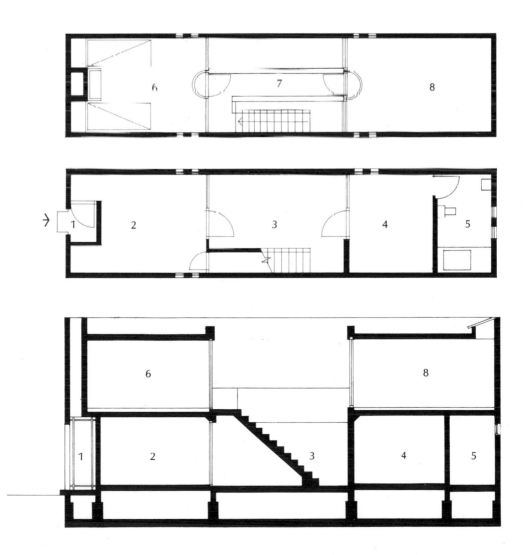

14 Looking towards the main entrance lobby from the living room

The first evident result of this decision is a clearer, more efficient plan: rooms are larger and better organized. But the effect of the change acquires a deeper significance when one considers its influence on the everyday activities of the inhabitants. The central court becomes an indispensable element of communication, linking directly the two living spaces at first level and, by means of a suspended deck, the master bedroom with the study bedroom at second level. In the total absence of windows on all external elevations, the open area acts as an intermediate space between interior and exterior and provides the only contact with the world of nature represented by air, light, wind and rain, which in turn play an important role in determining the use of the spaces opening onto the court. It is through this rather unique space that the elements of nature become part of the home and are inextricably bound with the ordinary acts of daily life.

15 Looking towards the light
court from the kitchen area

16 View of the dining area from
the light court; note the suspended deck that provides
shelter from the weather, and the
stairs leading to the upper level

17 The master bedroom

18 View of the upper deck linking
the two bedrooms

19 Looking from the master bedroom across the deck leading to
the study bedroom

The expression of the architectural idea,
however, is in marked contrast with tradition.
The architect's main intention was for the
solid mass of this enclosed building to stand in
relation to the neighbouring nagaya as an
example of conceptual art. It is meant to
provoke fresh thinking in terms of urban living
which, in the opinion of the architect, should be
influenced by tradition but expressed in a direct,
uncluttered manner suited to contemporary
lifestyles.

The structure of the house is of site cast,

reinforced concrete construction, with working
seams and formwork bolt-holes left exposed,
both outside and inside. Floors are covered with
slate tiles, on the first level, and timber strips on
the upper level. The choice of furniture reflects
the same principle that inspired the architectural design: practical yet elegant. Solid wooden
containers and tables are complemented by
early dining chairs by Hans Wegner, a designer
whose formative years were devoted to the
study of the traditional furniture of rural
Denmark. His chairs look in perfect harmony
with the proportions of these Japanese spaces.

A House in the Pinewoods of Tuscany, Italy

architects:
Giancarlo Bicocchi,
Luigi Bicocchi,
Roberto Monsani
project engineer:
Lisindo Baldassini
photography:
Carla de Benedetti

In the pinewoods of Roccamare, near Castiglione della Pescaia, a holiday home has been built which merges successfully with the landscape. In fact, nature and architecture are perpetually woven together and cannot be separated. The extent of the house is vague and undefined; the structure continues beyond the enclosure of space into the pinewood forest, and nature flows directly into the house itself. Pine trees grow up through the structural grid and the forest floor runs right up to meet the floor of the house. The trees dominate and shelter the house, filling it constantly with their noise.

The framework is constructed from hollow-section steel on a module of 2.72m (8'11") square. Columns support a grid that holds the panels with which the house is formed and reformed. Completely separate from this grid is the roof, made of self-supporting profiled aluminium sheeting on raised beams which occur at 5.44m (17'10") intervals. The rooms of the house are formed by a

20 View of the house amongst the trees

21 Axonometric

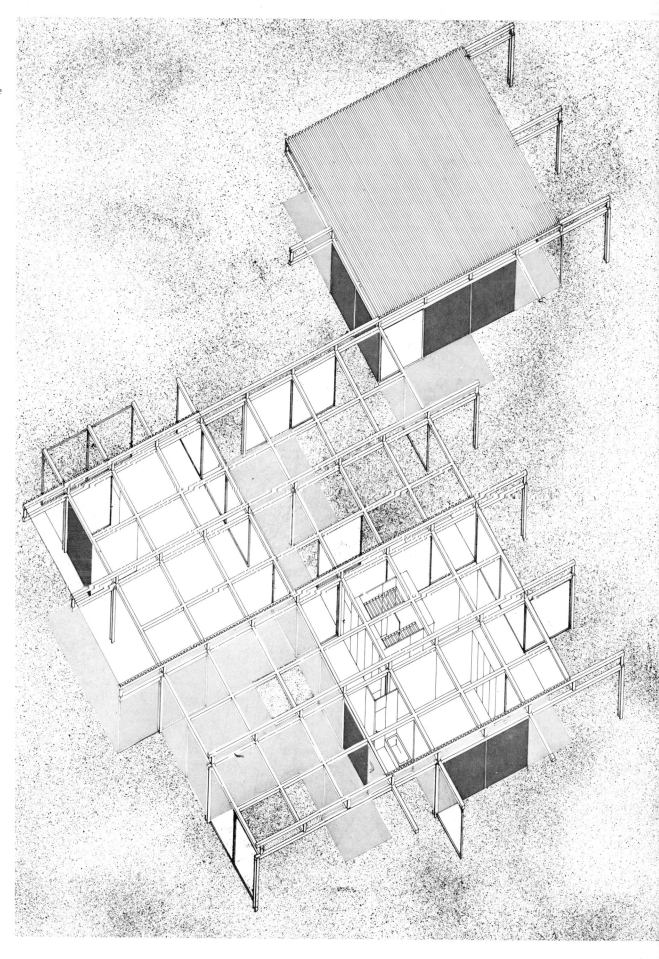

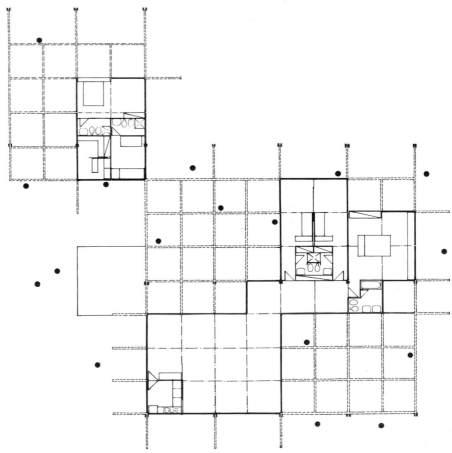

22 View showing roof
construction

23 Looking towards the woods
from the living area; note a
square of grassed area and a pine
tree, to the left

24 Plans showing some spatial
variations made possible by moving the gliding wall panels

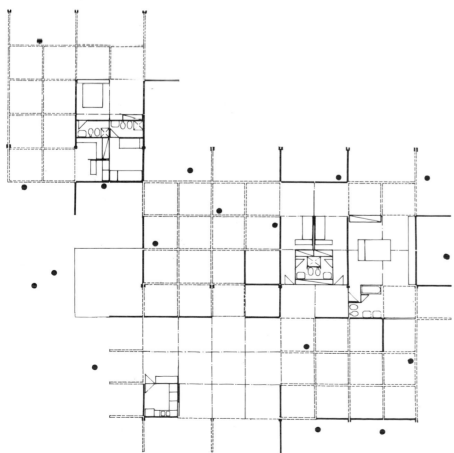

system of gliding and fixed frames into which are inserted opaque or smoke glass panels. The opaque panels, made from a sandwich of PVC laminate, with a core of polystyrene for thermal insulation, define three main, partially enclosed areas containing five bedrooms, with their related bathrooms, the kitchen and fixed storage containers which function as partition walls. The arrangement of the spaces around these rooms can change dramatically by gliding the panels on their external tracks. By this means, new vistas of the pinewood can be opened up and different internal spatial experiences created.

Ceiling panels are also of sandwich construction, with 12cm (4¾″) polystyrene insulation and a

waterproofing layer . All PVC surfaces are matt white inside and black outside. The floor is covered with 12cm (4¾″) wide timber planks which run through to the outside of the house. On the exterior paved surfaces the varnished planks are set apart to allow rainwater to drain away via concealed channels. Areas of grass occur within the house, often with a pine tree emerging from them. This weaving together of

boarded areas and grassed areas further reinforces the link between the exterior and the interior of the house.

Furniture is kept low and very simple, to allow the views into surrounding trees to dominate the interiors. Perspex coffee-tables and chairs, made by Acerbis of Italy, almost disappear into the greenery.

25 Another view of the living
space

26 Looking out to the woods;
note the open air swimming pool

Twin Dunehouses at Atlantic Beach, Florida, USA

architect:
William Morgan Architects
photography:
Creative Photographic Service
Alexandre Georges

The idea of building underground dunehouses along the beach originated from a desire to preserve the characteristic landscape for the neighbouring houses, built above ground to the north and south. However, the outstanding solution reached by William Morgan offers fresh argument in favour of those architects and ecologists who, concerned with the preservation of our physical environment, question the assumption that all domestic architecture should be built above ground. Also, the extent of coastal dune formation in this particular area would permit a large scale development without detracting from the original nature of the terrain – an important consideration at a time of increasing density of land use.

Each apartment contains 70m² (750 ft²) of interior space within a shell of Gunite, a cement mixture without aggregates normally employed for building swimming pools. The shape of the shell was designed by computer on a three dimensional coordinate system, and relies on sand backfill to post-tension the concrete for structural strength and stability.

27 A concrete drive leads to entrance to both units, recessed into the earth

28 Site plan

29 Computer analysis of structural shell

30 Plan
  1 Entrance
  2 Bathroom
  3 Sleeping balcony
  4 Kitchen
  5 Living area
  6 Terrace

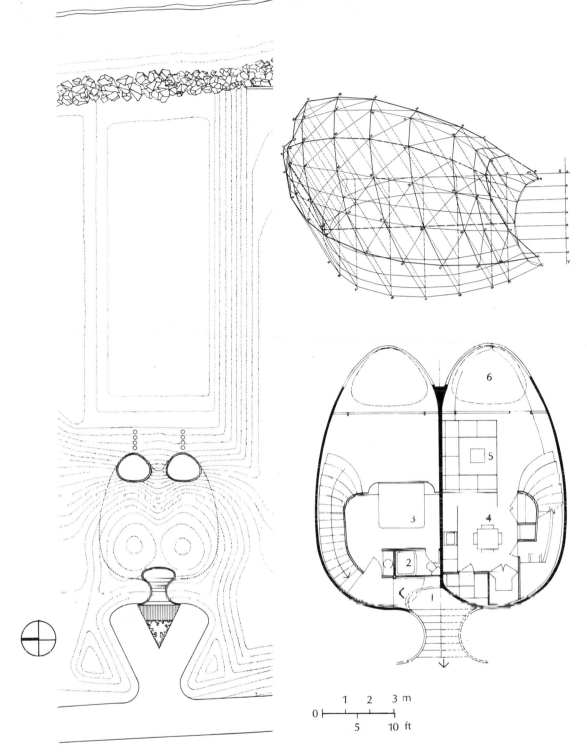

Construction was in two sections: first the lower part of the shell was installed within the excavated dune; reinforcing steel rods, inserted in the shell, were bent to the shape of the roof; then the 100mm (4") thick Gunite roof was applied over a plaster mesh. After two weeks the structure was waterproofed, the excavated sand replaced and green turf and vines were planted on top. Multiple shells could be built more economically by spraying a 60mm ($2\frac{3}{8}$") fibre-glass reinforced Gunite on air-inflated form bags. This method would reduce shell construction time from six weeks to three days,

and total construction cost to about 80% of conventional frame construction.

The entrance to each apartment is reached from the west, 6m (20') above sea-level, by a central staircase. From here a small lobby communicates with the sleeping balcony; then one descends a broad stair of increasing width, down to the single living space containing the kitchen and dining area, under the sleeping balcony, and the built-in seating in front of the glazed sliding door overlooking the sea. A small terrace provides shelter and at the same time

31 View of the two levels of one unit

32 Section of the two units, facing the ocean
    1 Storage
    2 Sleeping balcony
    3 Kitchen
    4 Living area

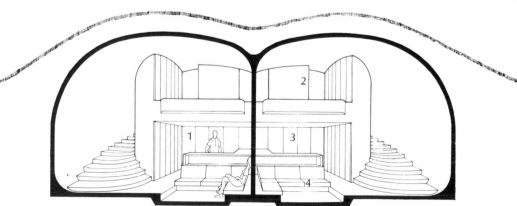

expresses the architect's intention of inviting the sea as near the house as possible. From the characteristic circular opening near the base of the dune, stepping stones lead directly on to the beach.

33 Detail of kitchen/dining area
beneath the sleeping balcony

34 The living area; to the right is
the glass door to the terrace

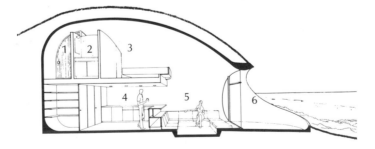

35 View from the sleeping balcony

36 Section of one unit
  1 Entrance
  2 Washing counter
  3 Sleeping balcony
  4 Kitchen
  5 Seating area
  6 Terrace

37 View of the twin terraces from the ocean side

The interiors express the contrast between the bearing concrete shell and the non-bearing timber structure. Wooden stair edges and partition tops are held away from the bearing shell to emphasise the architectural intent; this is further accentuated by concealed cove lighting. Such clarity of idiom plays a significant part in the feeling of opennesss that prevails in these structures built within the earth. The air conditioning and dehumidifying plant is operated by water cooled reverse cycle heat pumps. Fuel costs are about half those for conventional above-ground construction, due largely to the thick earth layer minimum 560mm (22") insulating the concrete shells.

The Vacation House of the Architect in Blokhus, Jutland

architect:
Claus Bonderup
photography:
Hedin
Claus Bonderup

The house is partly built underground, in a remote area of the west coast of Jutland rich in sand dunes covered with thick scrub. The undulations of the terrain practically hide the house from view: only two protruding glass bays can be seen from the beach, like a pair of goggles set in the direction of the sea. A narrow path, leading to one of two entrance doors, and a semicircular terrace were excavated with considerable concern for the natural contour of the land, so as to disturb as little as possible the wild character of the place.

The formula of a twin space projecting from a structural shell – a favourite idea of Claus Bonderup – presents some interesting variations in this project. Firstly, the twin space is contained within the dune with the exception of the extreme tips emerging above ground. The plan is then intersected by the alignment of the two entrance doors with a small central lobby. This creates a circulation pattern that acquires somehow the function provided by the traditional corridor: the kitchen and the dining areas are clearly separated, although they are both part of a single space, and might well

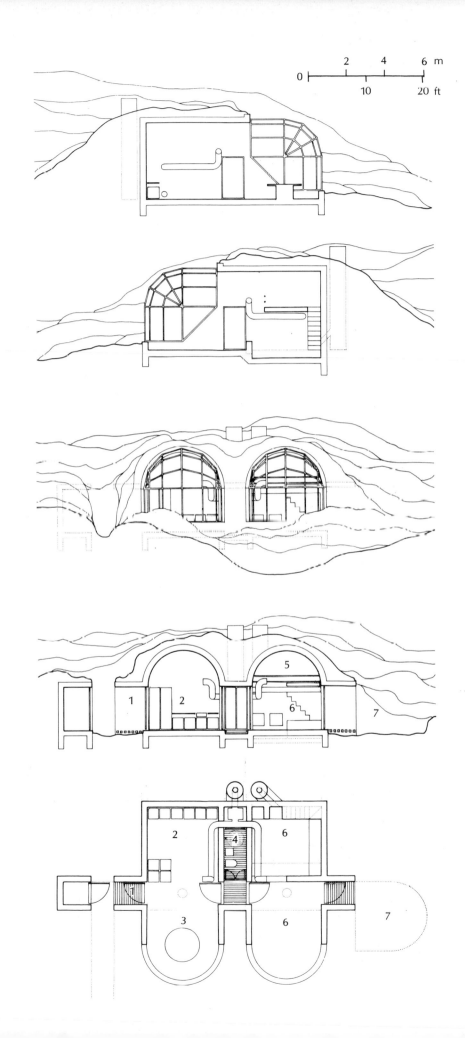

38 An aerial view of the dune-
house in its wild surrounding

39 Sections and plan
 1 Entrance
 2 Kitchen
 3 Dining
 4 Bathroom
 5 Sleeping balcony
 6 Living area
 7 Terrace

40 A view of the living area as seen from the sunken conversation area. The door to the left opens onto the terrace

be construed as an example of psychological space. When all doors are open one can walk across the entire house, from footpath to terrace; by closing the central lobby doors, the twin spaces become independent of each other.

The underground section of the building is a concrete shell with a vaulted roof to support the weight of the sand; the protruding bays are light structures of steel and glass. A central service core contains air conditioning and heating plant and the bathroom. In contrast with the kitchen and dining area, the lounging and sleeping areas were obtained with more structural means. By dropping the floor level at the back half of the space the architect obtained sufficient volume to construct a sleeping balcony over a sunken conversation area. Another structural element,

41 The conversation area and the sleeping balcony as seen from the glazed bay

42 A detail of the sunken conversation area

against the back wall, incorporates a neat fireplace for the conversation corner and a flight of steps leading to the sleeping balcony.

The furnishing is closely related to the architectural space, and designed to focus attention onto the landscape beyond the glass bays. Note how a free standing cupboard placed to the left of the entrance door helps to define the kitchen area. A pale grass matting along the passage way across the house emphasizes the circulation pattern; and the built-in storage, shelves and seating enclose the conversation area. Furniture, walls and floors are painted white, with a few vivid rugs to highlight the calm, serene setting. A most important element of decoration is given by the numerous semi-tropical plants that thrive in the even northern light, and in the heat provided by the ducted warm air system. The contrast between the luxuriant indoor vegetation and the wild scrub outside enhances the originality of this project.

43 The kitchen, opposite the dining area

44 An external view of the two glass and steel structures in deep snow; note, in the dining area, a banana plant apparently unaffected by the harsh climate

45 An aerial view of the Jutland coastline

The 'K' Villa on Lake Yamanaka, Yamanashi Prefecture, Japan

architect:
Shigeru Uchida
photography:
Yoshio Shiratori

This weekend residence of a graphic designer was built on the southern slope of the hill along Lake Yamanaka. The site is a well-known summer resort within one and a half hour's drive from Tokyo, and is famous for its magnificent views of Mount Fuji and of the lake. This particular house was planned so that it could be used for short holidays throughout the year.

Seen from a distance, the outline of the building belies the geometrical shape of the plan. Two asymmetrical wings appear to spread from a central space, giving an impression of lightness and dynamism that are enhanced by the slope on which the house stands. On closer examination, one discovers that the free form of the building is in effect the design solution of the problems faced by Shigeru Uchida in this project: the treatment of exterior space within the interior, and the special relationship between such an interior and the space surrounding the building.

The basic rectangular plan is modified at the second level by two timber structures that curve in

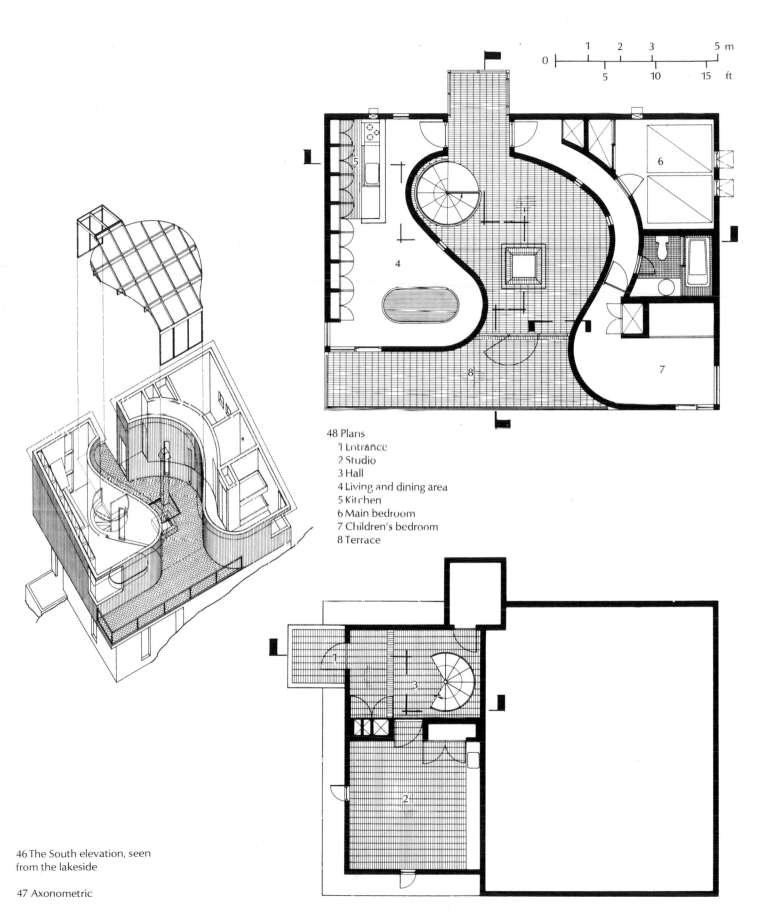

1 2 3 5 m
0 5 10 15 ft

48 Plans
1 Entrance
2 Studio
3 Hall
4 Living and dining area
5 Kitchen
6 Main bedroom
7 Children's bedroom
8 Terrace

46 The South elevation, seen from the lakeside

47 Axonometric

49 Looking up from the spiral staircase

50 The glazed recreation area is at the heart of the house between the day and night areas contained within the curving timber structures

convex and concave movement at the centre, as if attempting to enclose an outer area between them. Had this idea been followed through to the end, we would be looking perhaps at a house with a central courtyard; but in this case the solution is subtler. The outer space 'escapes' at two points, and the whole building acquires the fluidity of shape and the dynamic quality that are its distinguishing characteristics.

In order to integrate exterior with interior the architect resorted to glass. A steel frame construction that covers most of the central space was fitted between the two wooden structures of timber stud frame construction. The frame, glazed with insulating glass panes

fixed on a subframe, includes a glass door that opens onto the terrace. The function of this central space is manifold: it is both the entrance hall to the house and a transition between day and night areas. But it has a special importance as a recreation room, designed for the fullest possible enjoyment of nature. Note the simple fireplace, around which people can gather and relax, and the ingenuity of the hood and flue supported midway by the steel frame, the whole thing suspended between inside and outside to emphasize the close relationship between the two. Also, the central space provides daylight to the rest of the house through long narrow slits in the wooden walls. This solution, coupled with the sinuosity of the wall design, produces interesting light effects inside.

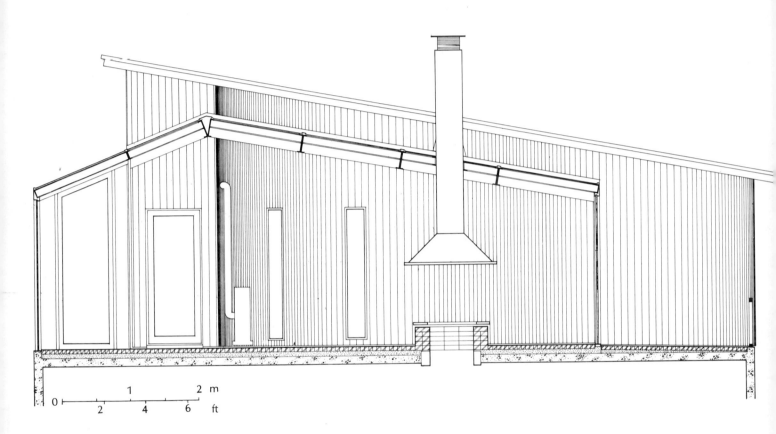

51 Sections and detail of junction between timber frame construction and the steel and glass structure over the recreation area
1 Stud
2 Timber facing
3 Steel mullion
4 Fixed glass panel
5 Door frame
6 Glass door panel

The main entrance, at first level, is decidedly understated. All that can be seen past the threshold is a spiral staircase leading to the second level and a door opening onto the designer's studio. Construction is reinforced concrete at its barest, with a brick floor. As one progresses upwards, however, the lovely shapes 'unfold' and at the same time the materials become lighter and more sensitively used: cedar wood panelling first; then, most naturally, glass. The arrival point of the staircase is marked by a glazed veranda that protrudes from the basic rectangular plan. At either side of the veranda, two doors lead to an open plan dining, living and kitchen area and, opposite this, to the bedrooms.

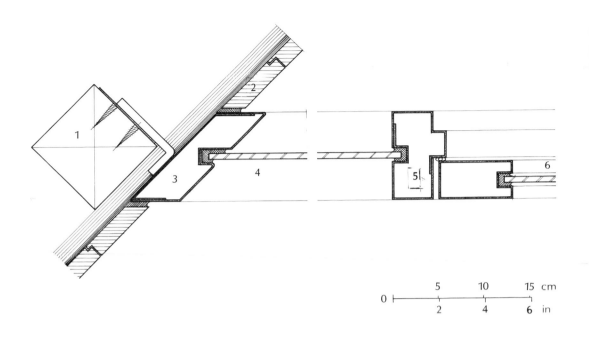

0 | 5 | 10 | 15 cm
2 | 4 | 6 in

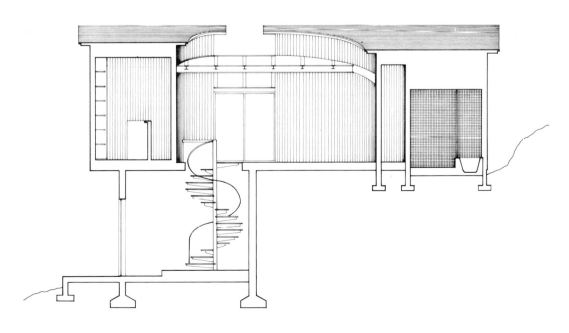

52 The kitchen area is little more than a counter, but is complemented by a triple range of storage cupboards

53 The dining pit

54 Another aspect of the dining/living area, with a view of Mount Fuji in the background

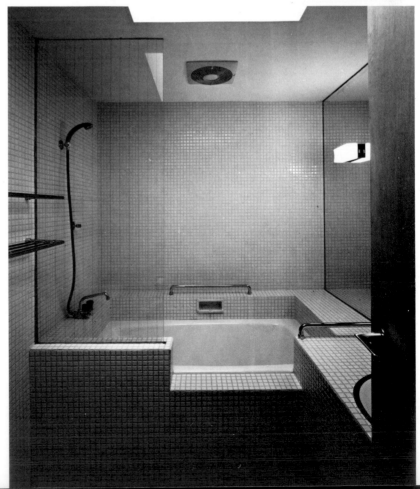

55 Children's bedroom

56 Bathroom

57 An exterior view of the house during late Autumn. Note how the colours blend with those of the natural surroundings

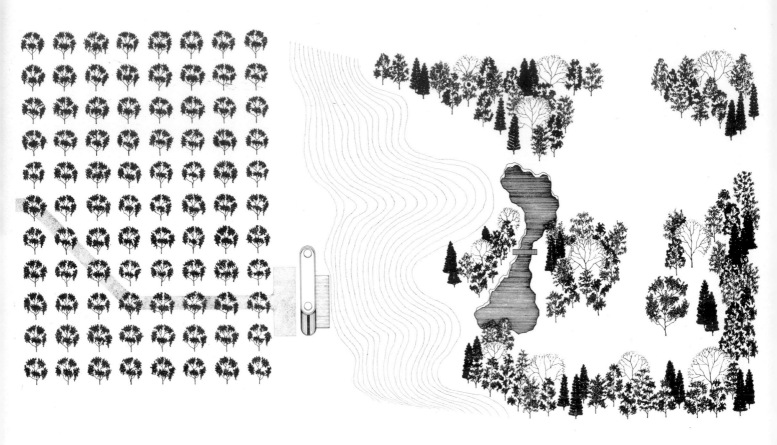

The Hot Dog House in Harvard, Illinois, USA

architect:
Stanley Tigerman & Associates
photography:
Philip Turner and
Williams & Meyer Company

This weekend vacation house is used throughout the year, and was named The Hot Dog House after its unusual proportions: 20m × 4.6m (65' × 15'). The site, a 4 ha (10-acre) plot bordered by a high-speed road, is rolling and wild with huge trees and offered very good opportunity for an imaginative use of natural landscape. The architect responded by introducing an individual element of fantasy and created a complete environment that contributes to the enjoyment of architectural landscape in a way that is culturally exciting.

The house was built in the vicinity of a brook that flows into a depression of the terrain which was extended and excavated to form a pond. The path to the house leads through a formal apple orchard consisting of 132 trees of the same variety, planted in a strictly geometric pattern. At the end of the path one is confronted by an opaque wooden wall with a single opening: the entrance to the house. The disconcerting neutrality of such a facade is wholly intentional: the architect imagined the front of the house to be as the proscenium of a stage, and the rows of trees to

58 Site plan: the apple orchard
forms a perfect screen between
the highspeed road and the house

59 The front of the house

60 Plans of first and second level

61 Looking up to one of the circular skylights from the first level; note, behind the stove, the ventilation louvre controlled by shutters

62 View of the informal dining
area from the sleeping deck

symbolise the audience. The curved jambs of
the door, a stylised version of the half-opened
theatre curtain, invite the visitor to penetrate
beyond the wooden wall and to step, via the
house, into Nature: across the sundeck, down
the bank, to the pond and into the wide open
country beyond. Looking back towards the
house, however, another unexpected, sudden
change of mood will be experienced as the
enigmatic mood of the facade is matched at the
back by a brilliant composition of two-

dimensional planes of colour and of translucent
glass, set in the controlled pattern formed by the
window frames and the ventilation grilles.

The building is mainly of timber frame
construction with a flat roof. A reinforced
concrete service core includes the kitchen and
two bathrooms. External and internal walls are
of cedar planks left untreated. Lighting and
ventilation problems that might have been
caused by the absence of windows on the south

63 The dining area as seen from the kitchen; note the straightforward treatment of the ceiling joists and the lighting, by silver capped bulbs

64 The conversation area; view taken from the seating bench encircling the iron stove

65 The north elevation of the house reflected in the pond

elevation were solved by building the upper floor as a suspended deck and by opening two circular skylights at both ends of the roof, over the voids at either sides of the sleeping deck. A system of louvred openings runs longitudinally at both ends of the house and alternates with the glass panes set in the timber frame of the

north elevation. Heating is by warm ducted air, fuelled by a large iron stove. The furnishing is simple and informal: semicircular benches built-in at both ends of the ground floor and covered with a vivid cotton print, 'butterfly' chairs, simple tables, rush matting on the wooden floors.

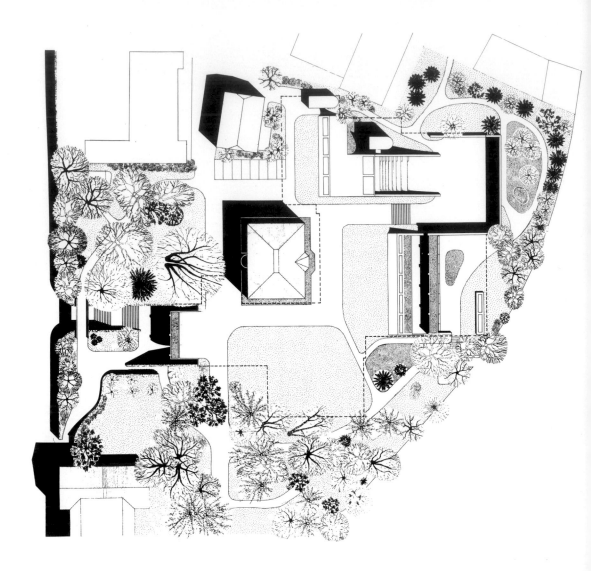

The International Museum of Horology at La Chaux-de-Fonds, Switzerland

architects:
Pierre Zoelly and
Georges-J. Haefeli
photography:
Henri Stierlin
Georg Stärk

The site chosen for the Museum of Horology at La Chaux-de-Fonds was the city park, a much valued site, where two protected buildings already existed: the Art Museum and the History Museum. In addition to 2000m² (21,500 ft²) of exhibition space, a conference hall, restoration workshops and a technical library were needed – a total area of 3770m² (40,600 ft²). Considering the sheer size alone, a conventional building would have entailed the destruction of the park. The obvious alternative was to build extensively underground. This in itself did not present exceptional technical difficulties, but it did require unusually detailed initial planning and a rigorous co-ordination of the different stages of construction. Decisions on structure, plan and underground levels were determined by strictly technical considerations. For example, a great deal of research went into designing a strong and flexible ceiling that could also be organized into a modular system, to economise construction time; underground levels were exactly calculated to reconstitute the original shape of the terrain; and location of the underground spaces, grouped into an apparently 'free' plan, was in effect determined by the necessity of avoiding the foundations of the historical buildings and the roots of mature trees.

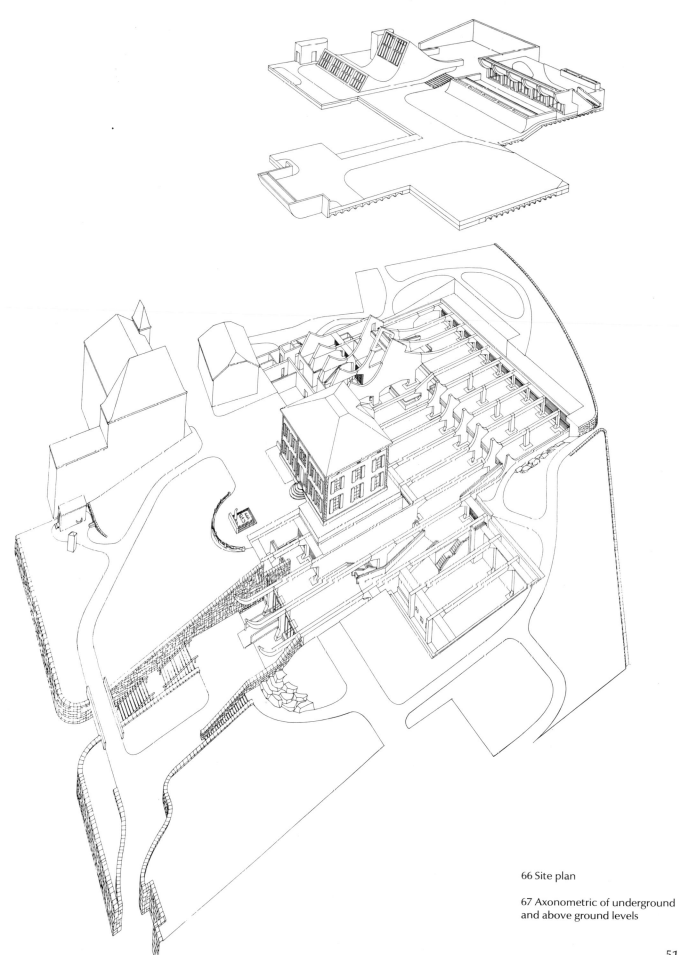

66 Site plan

67 Axonometric of underground
and above ground levels

68 Lower level; under the bridge, to the right, is the multi-purpose hall

69 View from the entrance hall, showing one of the bridges

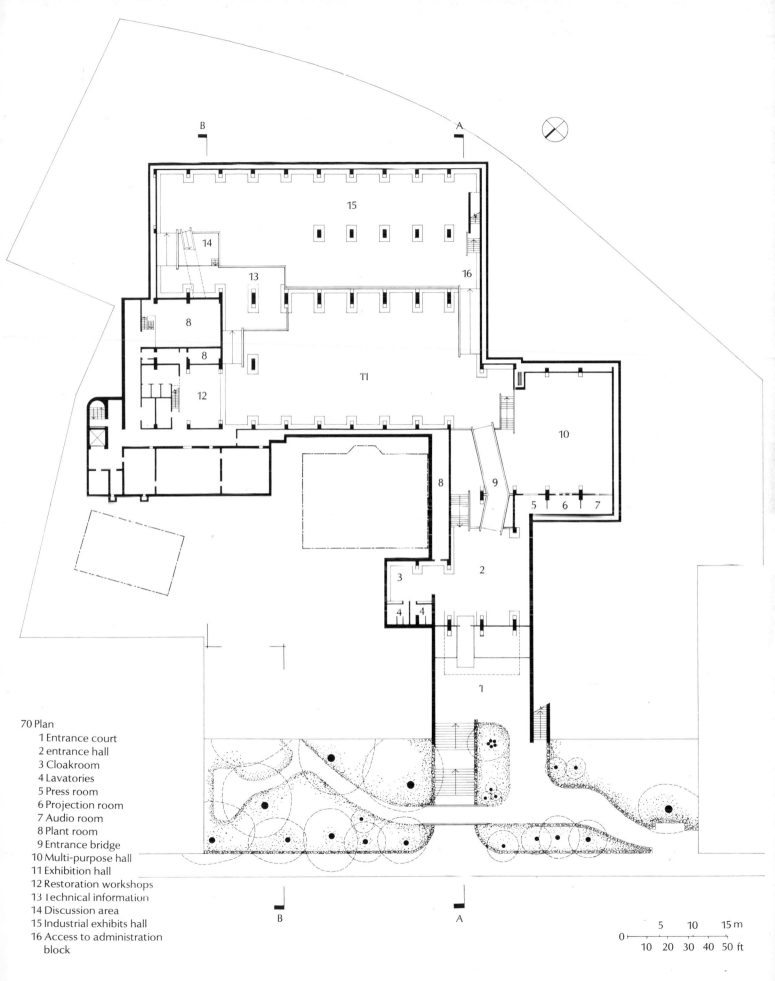

70 Plan

1 Entrance court
2 entrance hall
3 Cloakroom
4 Lavatories
5 Press room
6 Projection room
7 Audio room
8 Plant room
9 Entrance bridge
10 Multi-purpose hall
11 Exhibition hall
12 Restoration workshops
13 Technical information
14 Discussion area
15 Industrial exhibits hall
16 Access to administration
   block

5   10   15 m
0
10 20 30 40 50 ft

71 View from below ground exhibition hall showing workshops area; in centre of illustration is one of the purpose-built exhibition cabinets

72 Upper exhibition area; note the modular vaults and the four-track electrical installation; to the left is the bridge leading to lower level exhibition area

73 Constructional section
  1 Topsoil
  2 Felt filter
  3 Gravel
  4 Asbestos cement sheet
  5 Sand
  6 Damp proof membrane
  7 Thermal insulation
  8 Vapour barrier
  9 Screed over prefabricated
     units
 10 Prefabricated ceiling units
 11 Brick slips
 12 Bitumen roof finish
 13 Screed
 14 Fairface concrete
 15 Drainage channel
 16 Railway sleepers
 17 Sisal carpet tiles
 18 Reinforced concrete floor
     slab
 19 Over-site blinding

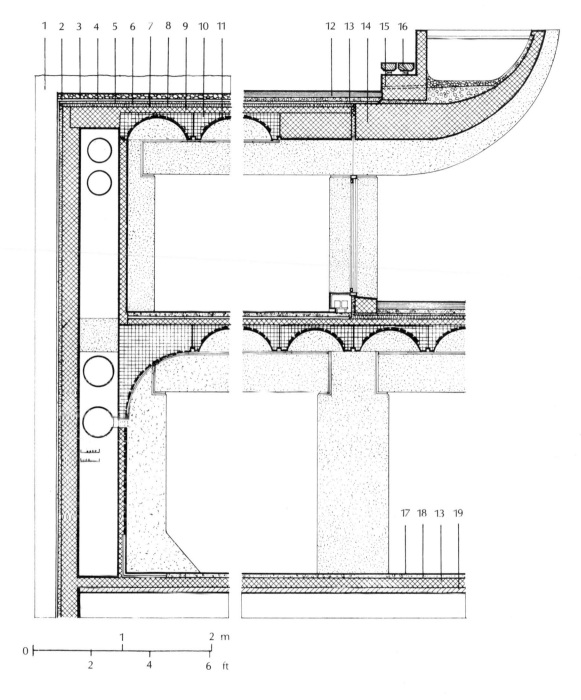

The original hill, which the Museum was to replace, was excavated through a breach in the old retaining wall along the 'rue des Musées'. Then a reinforced concrete structure, consisting of modules shaped like an inverted 'T', placed at 5m (16′ 5″) intervals, was cast on site and covered with a prefabricated skin of 400 modular vaults, faced with brick slips. The design of the structure above ground is based on the original land formation: a slope of 15% to the north, balancing the southern slope of the 'new town' built after the fire of 1794.

The plan is marked by three main accretions on the otherwise simple exterior wall outline. These give rise to internal corner conditions which present a considerable water infiltration problem because of the build-up of water pressure. As a means of controlling this seepage, the architects completely surrounded the building by a perimeter duct, which also serves as a full height service duct carrying electrical and air-conditioning installations. As an additional advantage, the duct protects and insulates the interior from the soil. Services have been

74 Looking up to the astronomy balcony from the transition area between workshops and industrial exhibitions hall

75 Open spaces over the astronomical exhibition wing; on the background is the administration wing

76 Roof shapes: the astronomical wing, left, and the workshops

incorporated in ceiling and floor structures, and a 1.6km (1 mile) long, four-track 'Lytespan' installation, strong enough to support hanging exhibition cabinets and panels, runs longitudinally between the vaults and bears lighting, loudspeaker, fire detection and alarm systems.

Any significant atmospheric changes would harm the precious mechanisms of the watches; so a constant interior temperature of 24°C with 55% humidity in Summer, and 20°C with 45% humidity in Winter had to be obtained. On the other hand, the considerable heat emanating from human bodies and incandescent lamps

77 Entrance to the underground
structure cut into the original hill

78 View of open space between
the astronomical wing, left, and
the administration wing

required a continuous change of air and a
heating and cooling system that could
counteract the rigours of the harsh winter
climate of the Jura. Here again, the decision to
build underground proved a wise one: excellent
insulation, and the heat provided by piped hot
water produced by the city refuse processing
plant, help to create favourable conditions for a
selective air-conditioning system. Three distinct
installations, serving different zones in the
museum, process a variable supply of fresh air
from a common intake; the air is then injected

through the perimeter service duct and
extracted via a central channel placed in the
floor between the industrial and craft display
areas. Spherical cabinets containing the more
delicate items have been specially designed to
ensure that the inside temperature and humidity
match that of the room. Materials have been
used with natural finishes throughout: fairface
concrete and bricks, for the walls, sisal
carpeting, glass and acrylic laminate for the
exhibition cabinets, anodised aluminium for the
halogen lamps and railings.

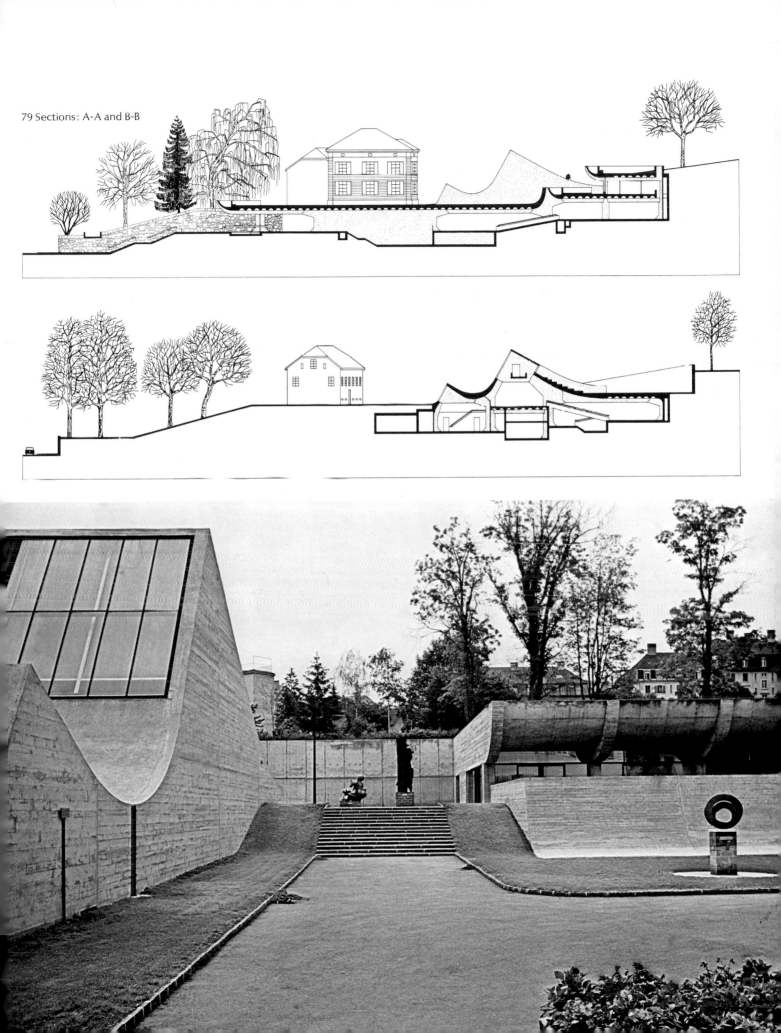

79 Sections: A-A and B-B

The Ingot – A Coffee Bar
in Kitakyushu, Japan

architect:
Shoei Yoh
photography:
Yoshio Shiratori

At first sight, the unusual appearance of this coffee bar leaves one rather perplexed. It looks like a scaled-down model of a skyscraper which, having been dropped on its side, had begun to sink slowly and inexorably into the earth until some mysterious underground obstacle arrested its progress, saving it from total burial. We are in effect observing the result of an ingenious combination of modern technology and basic engineering, that generates its own special type of beauty; an alluring beauty, deriving directly from the optical porperties of industrial glass.

A structural frame of 100mm × 30mm (4″ × 1¼″) steel joists on a concrete platform is entirely covered with Thermopane, a sandwich of two 5mm ($\frac{3}{16}$″) thick glass sheets with a 5mm ($\frac{3}{16}$″) air space fixed externally to the frame with a low modulus silicone mastic to allow for differential expansion and water-tightness. The inner sheet of glass is clear; the outer, a solar heat reducing mirror glass, has a chromium coating that gives it a highly polished and reflecting surface without complete loss of transparency.

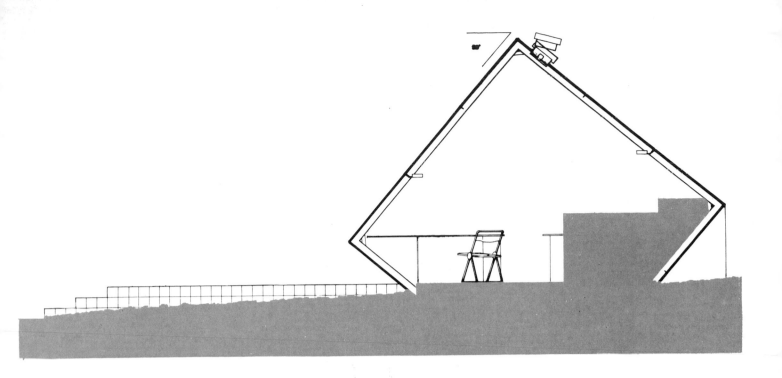

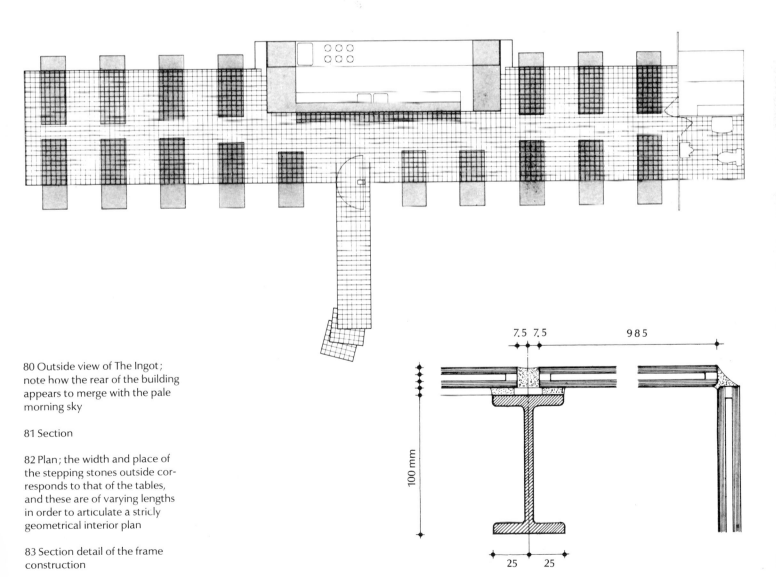

80 Outside view of The Ingot;
note how the rear of the building
appears to merge with the pale
morning sky

81 Section

82 Plan; the width and place of
the stepping stones outside cor-
responds to that of the tables,
and these are of varying lengths
in order to articulate a stricly
geometrical interior plan

83 Section detail of the frame
construction

84 The open door to the cloak-room; the wall is chromium coated like the outside of the building, and reflects the entire length of the inner space

The most intriguing effect of this logical and efficient concept is that the building acquires an uncanny dynamism. During daytime it plays a passive role, giving no hint of activity behind its facade that, like a huge mirror, reflects the sky and the surrounding trees. But as night sets in the whole structure comes slowly to life and the bright interior shines with a soft glow through the glass. A strong blue light illuminates dramatically the tiled pathway leading from the road to the entrance, and contrasts sharply with the white tiled floor and the glass interior.

The reverse seems to happen inside: the transparency is absolute during the day, but diminishes as darkness approaches. Only reflections are always present with endless variations, giving the illusion of new spatial dimensions as the pitched roof is reflected on the glass tables, or the Perspex and steel chairs

85 Detail of tables, made of plate glass panes glued with a special adhesive

86 The pitched roof mirrored onto the glass tables

are repeated ad infinitum on the slanted wall surfaces. Any artificial element of decoration would be out of place in such an interior; but series of delicate green ferns are arranged along both sides of the long space, and pick up the subtle shades of green and blue of the glass planes. The tables, designed by the architect, are glass panels fixed together with Photobond 100 adhesive, used experimentally by Shoei Yoh for some time (see, among others, *Decorative Art and Modern Interiors 1978*, pp. 178–179). The Italian 'Plia' chairs designed by Giancarlo Piretti for Castelli, look absolutely right in this setting.

87 Detail of the building at night; compare with illustration no. 80

88 Night view: contrasts of light and colour

A Solar House near Albuquerque, New Mexico USA

architect:
Antoine Predock
photohraphy:
Joshua Freiwald
Antoine Predock

In designing this solar house architect Antoine Predock wanted to create a building that would be so much part of the New Mexican landscape that it could not be deemed to exist anywhere else. His success is due to a direct response to the site conditions, the surrounding topography and the climate.

The house lies locked between two small hills, slotted neatly into the landscape like a formation of rock. Entering the house from the north via an entry court, one is immediately aware of the extensive views to the west. The strong link between the house and its landscape is further reinforced by the terraces placed around the building which are closely related to various rooms in the house

The treatment of windows should be noted in particular. The entire south wall of the house is taken

89 The south elevation showing
the solar panels

90 Plan of upper level
  1 Deck
  2 Bedroom
  3 Roof terrace
  4 Solar collectors

91 Plan of lower level
  1 Entrance
  2 Dining
  3 Living
  4 Terrace
  5 Kitchen
  6 Laundry
  7 Plant room
  8 Garage
  9 Swimming pool

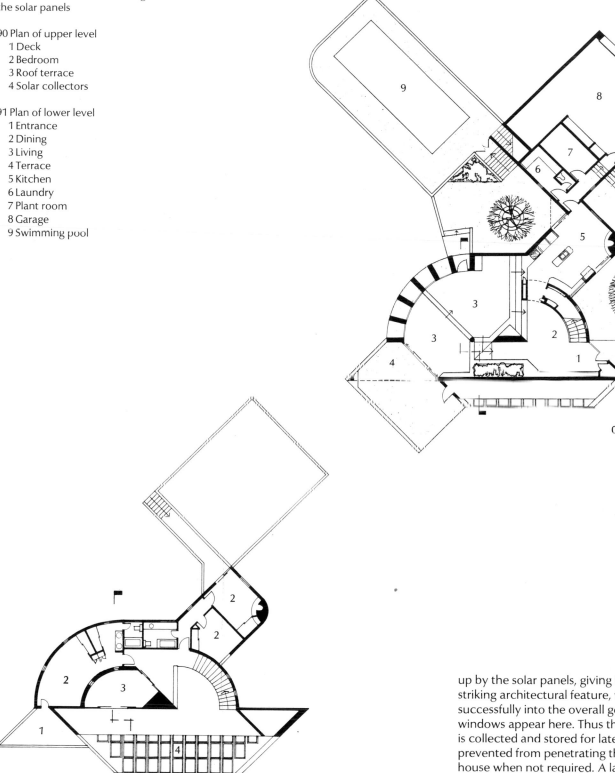

up by the solar panels, giving the house its most
striking architectural feature, which is integrated
successfully into the overall geometry. No
windows appear here. Thus the heat of the day
is collected and stored for later use and
prevented from penetrating the fabric of the
house when not required. A large window in the
southwest wall of the living area, which allows
views to the city below and the distant
mountains, is shaded from the summer sun by a
terrace off the master bedroom above and yet
allows the afternoon winter sun into the room.

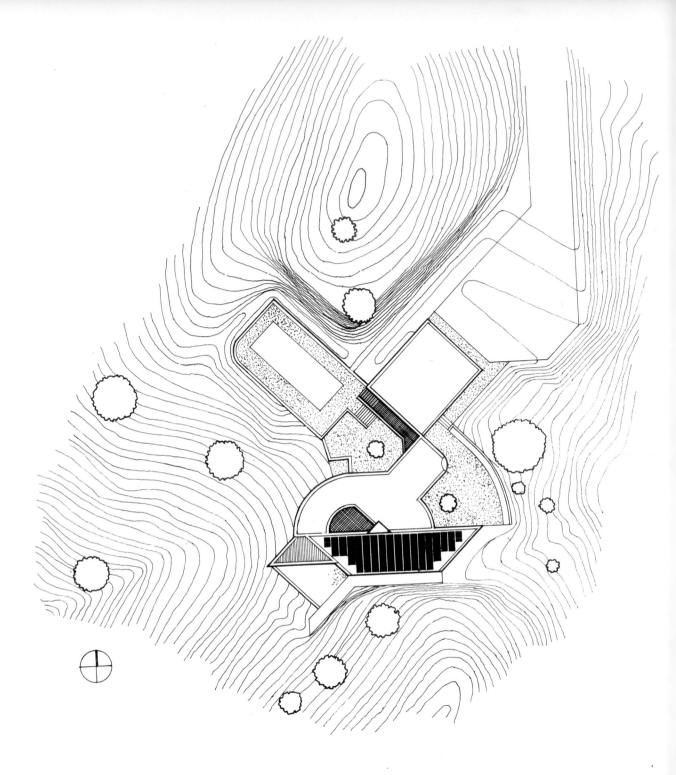

Radial fin walls shade the west windows but allow a view of the sunset. Other windows are small and kept to the shaded side of the building.

A solar house has to be considered as primarily a thermal machine rather than merely an enclosure of space. The first vital part of this machine is a heavily insulated form of construction, which in this case is provided by walls of 20cm (8″) or 40cm (16″) lightweight hollow concrete blocks filled with vermiculite and finished with 25mm (1″) stucco. This ensures

that the interiors remain cool during the extremely hot summer and warm during the cold winter months experienced at this altitude. The solar wall is formed by a series of flat plate collector panels, which are constructed from black steel piping connected to a backing sheet of black steel and faced with glass to trap and absorb the radiant heat from the sun. Through the piping runs a mixture of water and ethylene glycol (anti-freeze), which collects the heat from the panels. The now hot water runs through a heat exchanger where the heat is transferred to a secondary storage circuit. This circuit includes

93 Section
  1 Roof construction: 12mm (½")
    plywood on timber joists, with
    a Celotex layer under 4-ply
    roofing material
  2 Concrete fill
  3 Heat pump unit
  4 Wall construction: 25mm (1")
    cement stucco finish to
    pumice aggregate concrete
    block with vermiculite fill
  5 Quarry tile deck
  6 175mm (7") foil faced insulation
  7 280 × 420mm (11" × 16½")
    laminated beams
  8 18mm (¾") plaster on metal
    lath on timber studs
  9 Cement stucco finish
  10 Ground floor construction:
    brick on 100mm (4") concrete
  11 Solar collector panel
  12 50mm (2") urethane sheet
  13 50 × 152mm (2" × 6") tongued
    and grooved boarding
  14 50 × 203mm (2" × 8") joists at
    600mm (2'0") centres
  15 12mm (½") plasterboard

94 Diagram of solar system
  1 Solar collector
  2 Solar heated water loop
  3 solar heat exchanger
  4 storage water loop
  5 storage tank
  6 space heating exchanger
  7 space heating loop
  8 heat pump/coil
  9 domestic hot water exchange

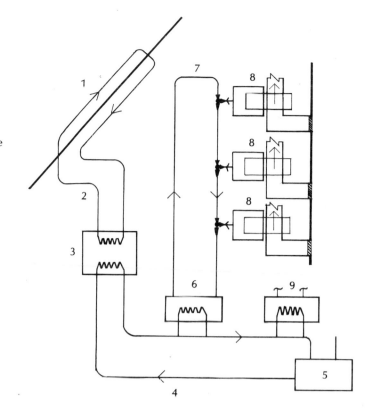

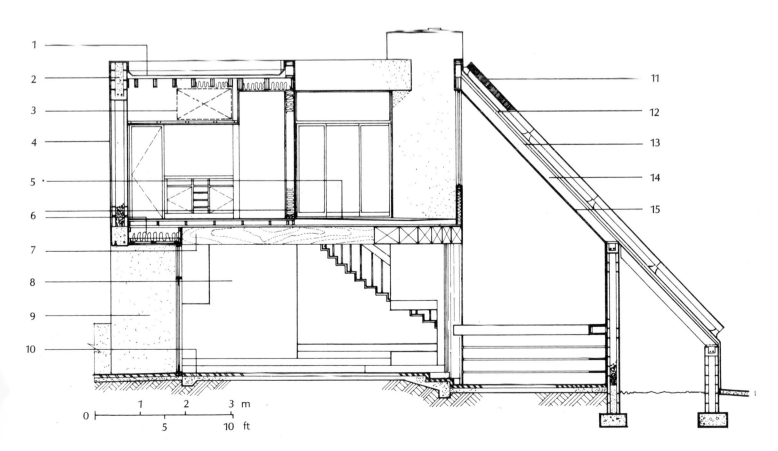

0 1 2 3 m

5   10 ft

95 View of the main living space
as seen from the entrance door;
the staircase leads to the
bedrooms

a 6000 gallon insulated storage tank placed beneath the driveway. The storage circuit then supplies heat to three separate circuits, again using heat exchangers. One heats the domestic hot water, the second feeds the warm air supply units while the third heats the water in the swimming pool. The pool itself can collect heat when not in use by means of an electrically operated black vinyl cover, which also prevents heat from escaping.

The solar system supplies 80 percent of the heat needed by the inhabitants. For additional heat there are three fireplaces and a backup electric heat pump. Natural ventilation is aided by the stepped building section and by the provision of high-level opening windows which, operating on the same principle as that of a chimney, create through ventilation.

A continuous cross reference between interior and exterior is expressed by the repetition of a basic shape that serves contrasting functions. Note for example how the design of the second level gallery in the main hall recalls that of the southwest veranda, which is in turn repeated in the shape of the fireplace in the living area. Ceiling and floor levels define the areas of the house, and the spaces possess a very clear identity that encourages a simple furnishing scheme.

96 Part of the living area; note the different floor levels and the characteristic timber ceiling radiating from a supporting column. Floors are of local brick, and absorb the heat from the low winter sun

97 Detail of main hall showing the sloping ceiling and a glazed area in the upper gallery wall

98 The southwest elevation

99 Looking west from the living area

100 View showing the remarkable integration of the house within the landscape

Hopkins House, Hampstead, London, England

architect:
Michael Hopkins
photography:
Tim Street-Porter
Michael Nicholson

An attempt by a property developer, to utilise commercially every square foot of an attractive site in the conservation area of Hampstead, was fortunately thwarted by one of those circumstances colloquially described as 'a down turn in the market': the developer had to sell the site, architects Michael and Patricia Hopkins bought it, and the planning authority, who regretted the previous consent to build two four-storey houses, gave eventually permission for a single, two-storey house of steel and glass.

The site, of 15m (49 ft) frontage with a deep garden, is in a comparatively low density street with graceful, early 19th century houses surrounded by trees – an improbable setting for a steel and glass building, one might suppose. But the architects took to their task with remarkable clarity of purpose, in a direct, uninhibited manner.

They wanted a house that could be occupied at minimum completion stage, so that details of the brief could be discovered while living in it. They needed a flexible house, that would respond to the

Glass wall head detail

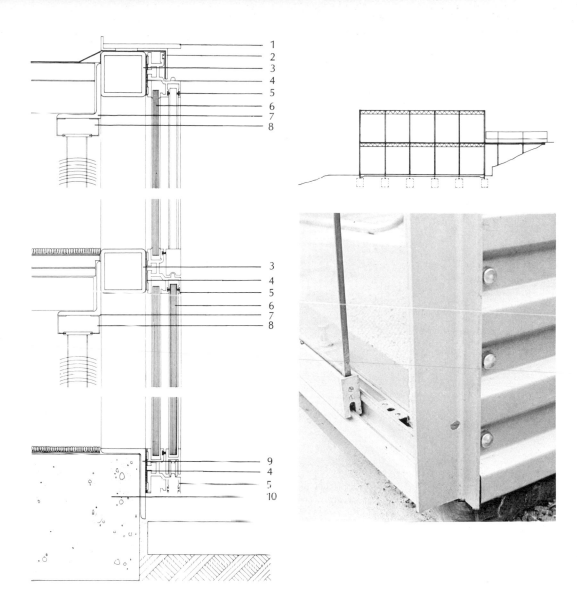

Glass wall intermediate cill

Glass wall base detail

101 The basic framework of the house is particularly evident in this view of the elevation

102 Sections of glass wall construction
  1 10 × 6mm aluminium plate
  2 43 × 43mm aluminium angle
  3 63.5 × 63.5 × 4.9mm Rolled hollow section
  4 Isolating tape
  5 Extruded aluminium glazing section
  6 10mm toughened glass
  7 80 × 60 × 6mm steel angle
  8 Venetian blind
  9 100 × 64 × 7mm Steel angle
  10 Concrete base slab

103 Section A-A

104 Detail of frame construction at ground level

105 Detail of roof construction

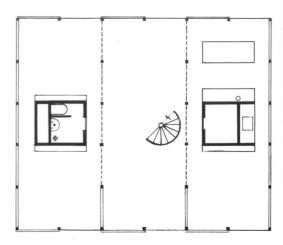

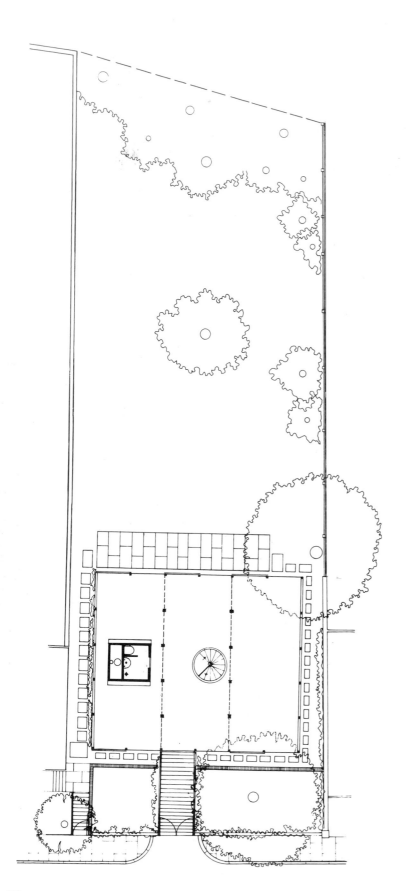

changing needs of two professional parents and
their three young children. Thus the upper
storey, at street level, would initially be used as a
studio for the parents' architectural practice
while the lower storey, opening onto the garden,
would be the family home. As the children grew
older, the studio could be moved somewhere
else and the house would be separated into
parents and children's flats.

As can be seen, a great deal of experimentation
was an essential part of this approach. The
architects carried this further when they
decided to utilise components and technology
developed for larger industrial buildings and
reduce them to a domestic scale. Finally, by
using very simple constructional details
repetitively, and by managing the contract with
direct labour and specialist subcontractors, they
wanted to find out, in their own words, 'how
much can we get for how little'. The cost,
calculated at the rates current between August
1975, when work was started on site, and April
1976 when the house was first occupied, was
just under £20,000 for a building area of 230m²
(2,500 ft²) including all internal finishes and
fittings.

The structure is a light steel frame on a 4m × 2m
(13′ 1″ × 6′ 6″) grid with 63mm × 63mm
(2½″ × 2½″) columns and 250 mm (10″) deep
lattice trusses supporting both the first floor and
the roof. The frame is stiffened with 50mm (2″)
decking to the floor and roof. Apart from the
flank walls, made of two skins of profiled metal
cladding with fibreglass insulation infill, both the
street and garden elevations are completely
glazed in 2.7m × 2m (8′ 10″ × 6′ 6″) panes, with
alternate fixed and sliding panes. A single
aluminium section was specially designed to
fulfill the different track conditions at eaves, first
floor and ground sill levels.

106 Plans at garden level and at hill level, and side elevation

107 Entrance at street level

108 Light effects through venetian blinds

109 A spiral staircase from main entrance level leads to kitchen and dining area

110 Another view of lower level showing the function of venetian blinds in relation to the entire space

111 The main dining area

112 One of two identical bath/
shower rooms, built on a concrete platform; walls and ceiling
are of plastic laminate joined
with a silicone mixture; the
shower water comes from an
outlet on the ceiling

113 Detail of bedroom area

114, 115 Two views of a paved area at the back and side of the house

116 Corner view showing contrasting effects of cladding and glass wall

The street entrance is approached by a small bridge over the garden, and opens directly into the office at the upper floor. With the exception of three non-structural enclosed spaces, for the two bathrooms and the kitchen, both floors are arranged as open plans. Interior finishes are absolutely minimal: the industrial components used for the structural grid have been left exposed, and from the lattice trusses hang venetian blinds which act as room dividers and provide complete privacy. A uniform, grey fitted carpet covers the floor. The furniture is essentially functional: groups of good chairs and tables help to define the use of space, but the conventional wardrobes and cabinets have been replaced by open shelves and by low containers running on castors. Lighting is by spot and floodlights on tracking, supplemented by floor and table lamps.

The Home of the Architect near Los Angeles, California, USA

architect:
Helmuth Schulitz
photography:
Carla de Benedetti

The opportunity to acquire a building plot of land with magnificent views of Coldwater Canyon, in Los Angeles, and of the distant sea, at a good price, would be an irresistible temptation for many. This plot was a difficult one however, with such a slope on it (40°), that it was considered almost unusable, and where both the design of the house and the methods of construction had to be adapted to the special situation, at a cost not higher than that of a more traditional house. In addition, Helmuth Schulitz decided to demonstrate some of his own concepts about building single or multi-family homes in California, about industrialized building methods, and about prefabrication.

The house is an attempt to maximise the use of prefabricated standard components within a system that is flexible enough to be adapted to the specific requirements of the user and to the characteristics of the building plot. This approach appears to be the reverse of what normally occurs in house building, when traditional methods of construction, requiring costly skilled labour, are used for standard designs that are sold as suitable for any situation. Total prefabrication on the other hand is inflexible and has numerous disadvantages, as for example the monotony of the types of

82

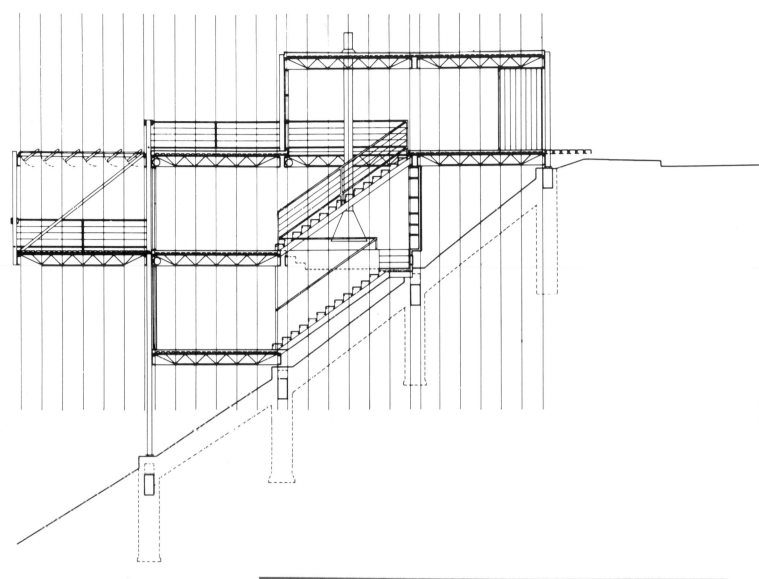

117 Side view of the house; note
the cellular frame characteristic
of the architectural plan

118 Section

119 Looking upwards the exterior
elevation

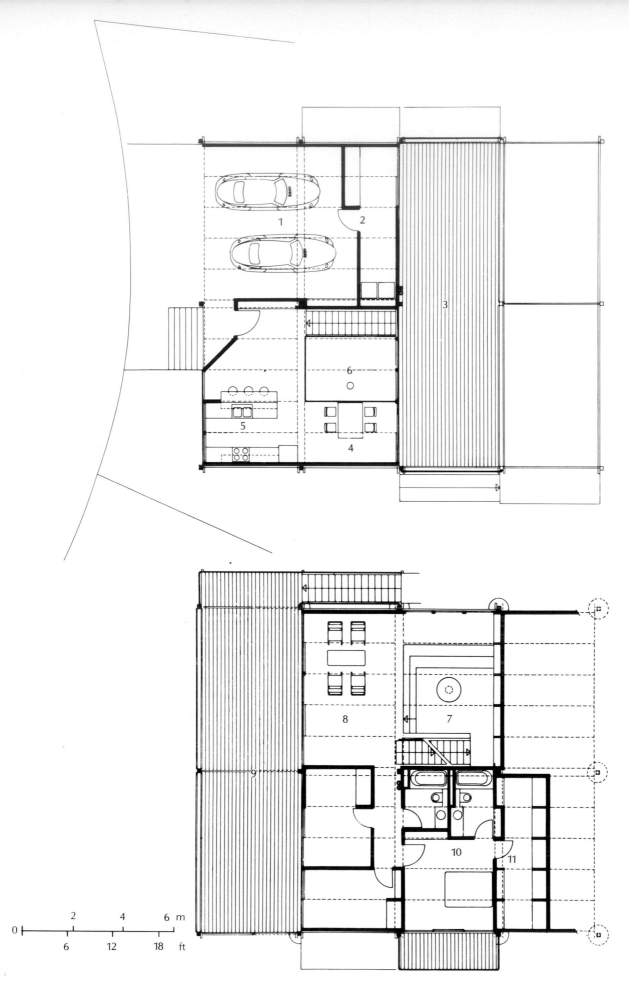

2   4   6 m

0

6   12   18   ft

layouts offered, the difficulty of adapting
standardized construction to environments
which necessarily differ, and the major capital
investment that total prefabrication requires. In
this instance, the architect built his model after
surveying the various industrial components
available on the market: structural elements,
panels of various types, windows, and so on. His
selection was made according to module sizes
and ease of integration between parts. He then
produced a catalogue of selected parts with
detailed indications on how to coordinate them,
which has become a designer's guide to an
extremely open and versatile construction
system.

The structural frame of the house is based on a
three-dimensional steel module, and rests on
cylindrical caissons. There are no load-bearing
walls; partitions are panels of aluminium with
layers of insulating material. Double glazed
sliding windows with aluminium frames reach
from floor to ceiling so that the landscape

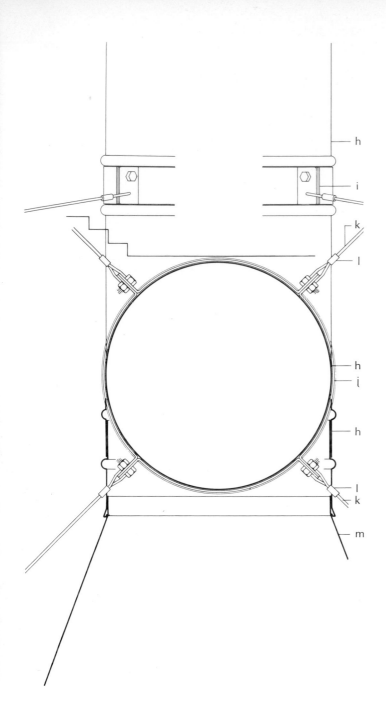

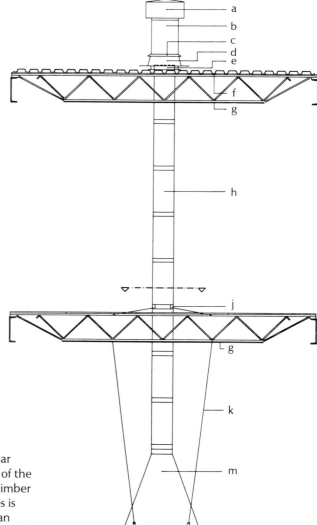

122 Section and plan detail of the suspended fireplace

123 View of fireplace over the conversation pit

becomes part of the interior. The modular structure of the house follows the slope of the terrain, and a projecting terrace with a timber plank floor and adjustable plastic louvres is accessible from the living room and by an exterior staircase. The house is open and well lit, the entire frame in full view and underlined with colour. On the street level are the entrance, the kitchen and the dining areas; from here, as if from a balcony, one looks down into the living room below. A metal staircase leads down. The ceilings are of prefabricated steel decking supported by a system of small metal trusses that span between beams.

124 The kitchen area

125 View of the veranda; note
the plastic louvres that can be
completely closed

An Apartment in Milan, Italy

designer:
Daniele Boatti
photography:
Carla de Benedetti

This conversion of an old apartment in the centre of Milan exemplifies an imaginative use of large spaces that avoids elaborate structural alterations. The owner, a wealthy industrialist, wanted a city flat that could hold his collection of modern paintings, antique furniture and art pieces. Although he had not been specifically trained in architecture or design, he did have a clear idea of what he needed so as to be able to design the conversion himself.

The lofty rooms of 19th century Italian palazzi are not easy to convert into modern spaces: their high ceilings and tall windows may appear rigid and uncompromising to the designer accustomed to the terse idiom of contemporary architecture. The most frequent solution, apart from building a suspended ceiling, is to divide the volume horizontally and thus create a mezzanine; but although this method does guarantee the most economic utilization of available space, the result is seldom pleasing. Questions of scale and proportions remain unsolved, and affect in particular a very

126 Looking from the dining area towards the entrance, which is screened by the partition to the left

127 Detail of bathroom

128 View of living area

sensitive architectural element: the window, which appears to suffer most from this drastic treatment.

Daniele Boatti used some of the existing spaces as containers for a light timber structure that recalls the basic post and beam frame construction of the traditional Japanese architecture. He animated the monotonous, too regular shape of the rooms by variations in floor levels and used a system of blinds, again reminiscent of Japanese interiors, to define smaller spaces and control the intensity and quality of light coming through the large windows. Artificial lighting, by spotlights fixed onto the timber beams, can be directed

downwards so as to leave the high celings in the dark and intensify the illusion of smallness. The presence of numerous paintings, attracting attention to specific points, might however result in a further, unwanted restriction of visual communication between areas. This is counter-acted by a bold use of skeletons of small exotic trees and bushes, preserved by a special treatment, which are placed against the walls and over the timber frame and, leading the eye upwards, restore the original proportions of the rooms without disturbing the spatial balance of the different living spaces. Their dark outline contrasts with the upholstery of the modular seating in the main living area.

129 View of living area and of raised area that can be screened by roller blinds

130 Plan

131 Detail showing the timber frame construction and the relationship between the raised area and the dining space

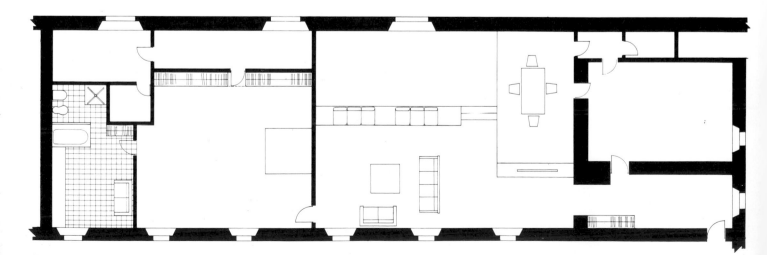

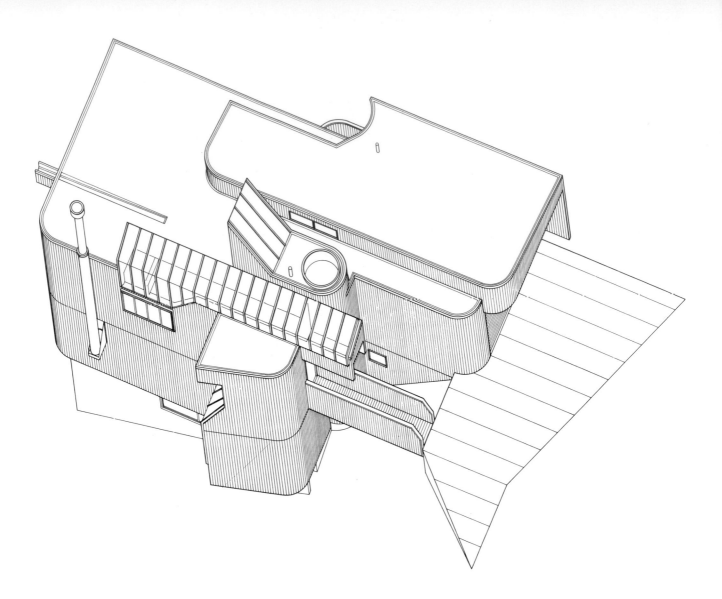

A House on Lake Washington, near Seattle, USA

architect:
Wendell H Lovett
photography:
Cristian Staub

This house for a couple without children is set on the eastern slope of a wooded island in Lake Washington. During the winter season the lake can be seen through deciduous trees to the south and east, while in summer the house is well screened by vegetation. The architect, a dedicated environmentalist, made full use of this particular feature of the site. The house is poised over the slope so that the views can be enjoyed from a prominent position; its shape is articulated into a variety of forms that produce sheltered outdoor spaces, variation in levels and interesting light effects inside.

The building is of timber frame construction over a concrete base that follows the declivity of the terrain, from the west carport down to the east elevation. Glazed areas, extensively developed on the south wall, are particularly effective when used as skylights. One of these is the long 'sky-slot' which extends from the entrance bridge across the living room into the study. Its reflective, segmented length is first seen through the trees as one approaches from the north, and rests lightly

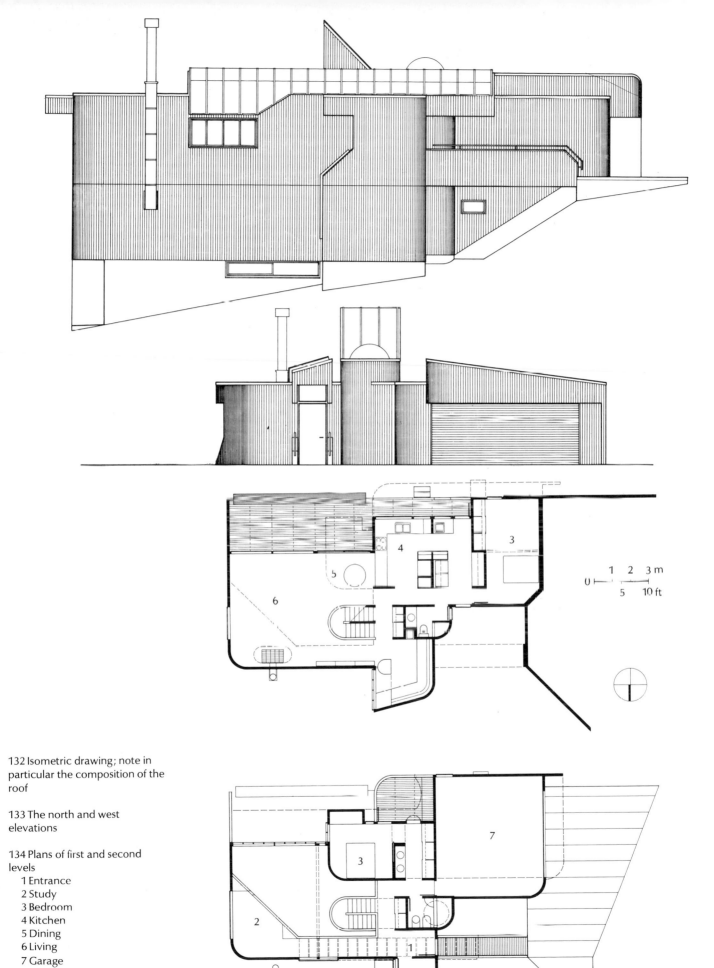

132 Isometric drawing; note in particular the composition of the roof

133 The north and west elevations

134 Plans of first and second levels
  1 Entrance
  2 Study
  3 Bedroom
  4 Kitchen
  5 Dining
  6 Living
  7 Garage

135 Main entrance bridge

136 Looking down from the study: to the living and dining areas, and to the suspended master bedroom above, left. Facing the bedroom wall is the entrance corridor

137 Another view of the main living space as seen from the landing outside the master bedroom; the helical shape of the stairs is the fulcrum of the entire space

on the closed, wrapping forms of north and west wall, drawing the eye from entrance bridge into the dwelling. Other transparent forms, such as the glass roof over the central stair and the large plastic dome above the master bedroom, animate a basically flat roof.

From the entrance bridge one reaches the upper level of a two-storey living space into which virtually all other spaces flow. The design of the interior is based on the functional use of an architectural volume repeated on a different

scale throughout the building. The solid, helical shape containing the open staircase and bath facilities on two levels is a pivotal element about which the major open areas of the house are defined. Another large solid element, adjacent to and in opposition to the stair volume, is the suspended master bedroom, its rounded wall projecting into the main living space from the upper level. Beneath the bedroom is the dining area. Kitchen, laundry and a guest room are below the dressing room and the garage.

138 Looking across the living space

The rounded container form is repeated within the major space in three smaller volumes. These are the fireplace hood, punctured by air convecting andirons; a vertical half cylinder, wall-mounted on pivot hinges, which contains television and audio equipment, and a horizontally cantilevered, half-cylindrical cabinet that partly screens the kitchen from the dining area.

Finishes are used uniformly throughout, according to function: oak floors for the living area and the bedrooms, glass mosaic tiles for the kitchen and bathroom. Walls are white-painted plasterboard; low ceilings and exterior cladding are red cedar finished with a preservative stain.

139 The fireplace is a design of the architect, and functions with air convecting andirons. Cool air is drawn in near the floor, is warmed as it passes through the 10cm (4") tubes, which are heated by combustion gases, and is exhausted into the room

140 The upper bathroom, with
light streaming through the
plastic dome on the roof

141 Outside view of the house

The Vasarely Foundation
near Aix-en-Provence, France

architects:
Jean Sonnier and
Dominique Ronsseray
photography:
Jean-Pierre Sudre
Fondation Vasarely

After searching for a suitable site for more than twenty years, Vasarely has, at last, built a centre for the study of his paintings in relation to architecture. He considered converting several historic buildings, but eventually decided that his avant-garde work would require a purpose-built, advanced building so that it could function with fewer constraints.

Vasarely's conception was to cover the facade of the Foundation with an alternating composition of black and white. The architects Jean Sonnier and Dominique Ronsseray turned this idea into reality. The Foundation stands on the crown of a smooth green mound near Aix-en-Provence. On the entrance front the building is reflected in an ornamental pond, while on the opposite side it is glimpsed through a screen of trees.

The building has to fulfil three main functions: firstly, to bring together forty-two monumental works

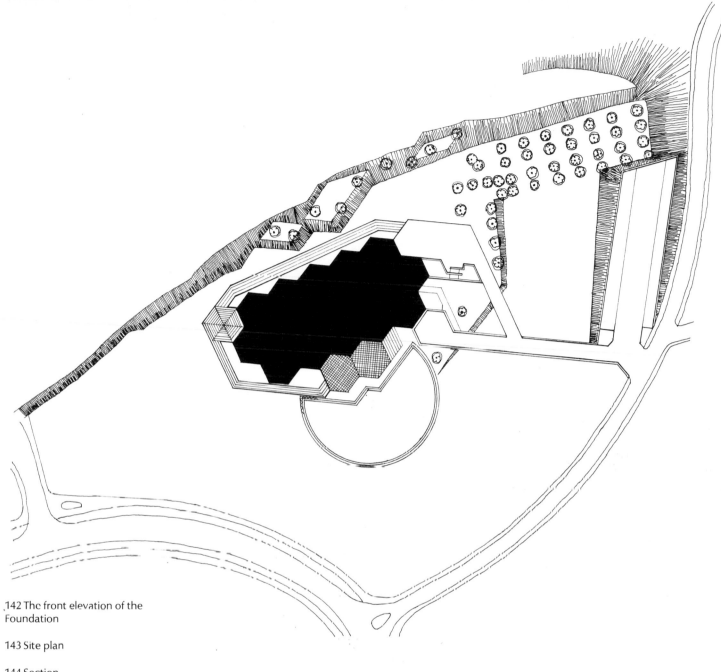

142 The front elevation of the
Foundation

143 Site plan

144 Section

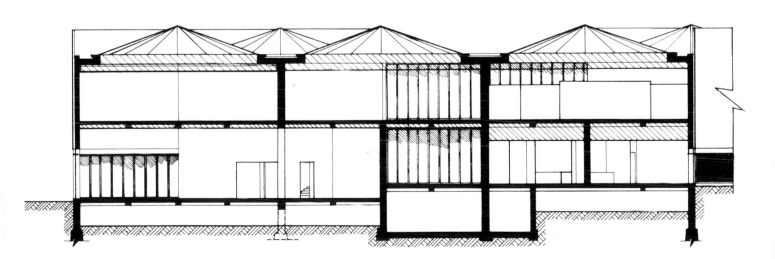

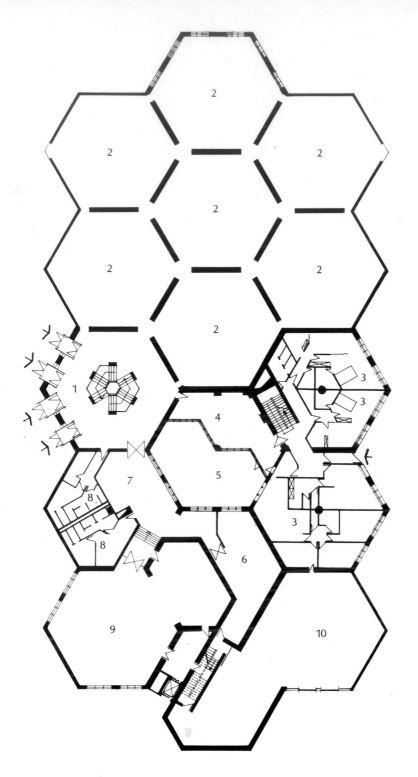

145 Plan
1 Entrance hall
2 Exhibition of paintings related to architecture
3 Staff lodgings
4 Bar
5 Patio
6 Library
7 Foyer
8 Cloakrooms
9 Seminar and lecture space
10 Maintenance workshops

147 View of the Foundation from the approach path; the main entrance is to the left

in the same exhibition space; secondly, to provide lecture rooms where the principles deriving from Vasarely's idea of integrating painting with architecture can be demonstrated using models and other audio-visual techniques; and thirdly, to collect and discuss research into these principles at conferences and seminars.

The administration rooms, library, archives and workrooms are all grouped around the conference room. These, in turn, are closely linked with the main exhibition hall and the other public areas. A modular system of interlocking hexagons expresses the unity of the various functions of the building on plan.

The modular plan has lent itself well to standardization of construction. The use of prefabricated concrete elements greatly shortened the time of erection. All the structural framework was standardised and the floor was constructed by the assembly of prefabricated triangular units, which were then covered with grey marble quarried in the Alps.

148, 149, 150 Three aspects of the exhibition space, showing details of the glass domes, left, and the spatial relationship between the cellular elements of the building. The seating system was especially designed by the Belgian designer Emile Veranneman

151 Some of the monumental
Vasarely paintings

152 Looking at the Foundation
through the trees at the back of
the building

The facade has been created by forming a
framework of grey anodised aluminium
members which runs right round the building
and masks the roof structure. Depending on the
function and requirements of the various
interiors, it is either fully glazed or fixed to an
insulated concrete wall and clad with
aluminium. Each of the distinctive black and
white panels is composed of 16 sheets of 6mm
($\frac{1}{4}$") gauge anodised aluminium. The panels seem
to float above a strip of glazing, which is either
opaque or transparent, with the exposed
framework forming the mullions and transomes
of the windows.

To achieve the required natural lighting the roof
structure springs off the hexagons into a
pyramidal shape using equilateral triangles of
glass in a framework of laminated wood. Each
triangle has a side of 1.45mm (4'9") and each
dome is composed of 96 triangles, covering a

total area of 100m² (1076ft²). Overhead lighting
brings with it the problem of excessive heat-gain
from the sun. Therefore, a laminated glazing
material was produced to counteract this: a
layer of aluminium net between two sheets of
toughened glass acts as a brise-soleil and
reduces the amount of infra-red light entering
the building. The laminated glass also suffuses
the light to prevent direct sunlight from falling
on the works of art.

The Foundation has a sophisticated, completely
electric air-conditioning system which can
either cool or heat the building. When
necessary, heat pumps recycle waste heat
extracted from the building. This type of air-
conditioning system requires a highly insulated
structure and the concrete wall construction
includes a layer of glass fibre to this specific
purpose.

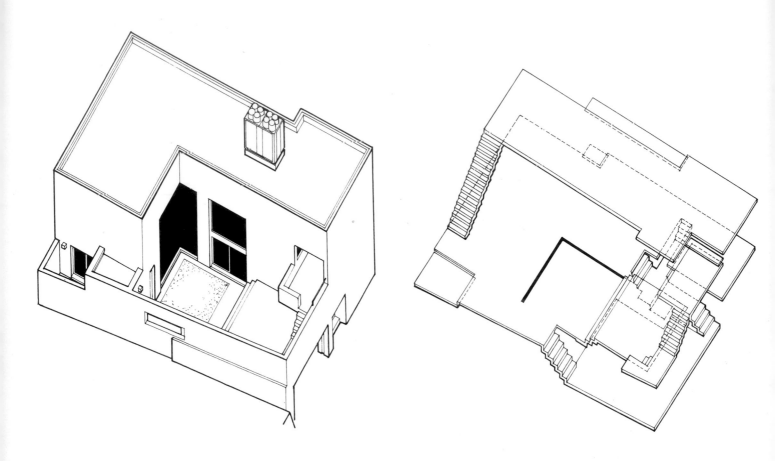

The Takahara Residence
in Tokyo, Japan

architect:
Masayuki Kurokawa
photography:
Yoshio Shiratori

The design of this house appears to be inspired by a duality of mode. Two equally important concepts are immediately apparent: that of space as volume, wherein openings, voids, and wall outline, represent the negative element of an architectural whole – its medium is the boundary between exterior and interior. The other concept is the continuity of interior spaces, realized by the repetition of lines of movement. This is symbolised by the stair, and applies both within and across the three levels of the house. Note in this respect the circulation pattern that links first to second level, or is confined within the second level alone; similarly, the third level has two main circulation patterns: one encloses master suite and child bedroom, the other includes the second level. The logical development of this scheme results in functional spaces being treated as 'alcoves' protruding at different levels from the central volume of the house. (See circulation plans.)

The realization of this very individual idiom is particularly successful at the second level. The boundary between interior and exterior is subtle and elusive: large areas of glass, used both for

153 Axonometric of the house
and of the structural elements

154 Plans of first and second level
    1 Garage
    2 Entrance
    3 Tatami
    4 Courtyard
    5 Passage
    6 Living room
    7 Dining area
    8 Kitchen
    9 Utility room
   10 Bedroom
   11 Master bedroom
   12 Terrace

155 Circulation pattern
    A Main living space
    a Dining alcove
    b Garden alcove
    c Bar alcove
    d Balcony alcove

156 North side elevation

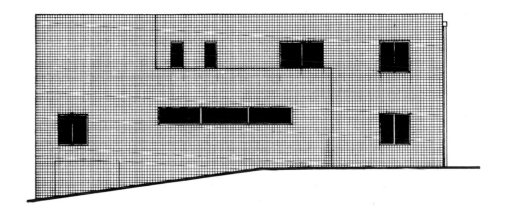

157 External view of the three levels

158 Detail of first level; note the double access to the house, by open stairs leading to the paved garden and, to the right, through the entrance door

159 From the narrow entrance passage there is an indication of the wide living space. The stone wall to the right separates the tatami room and the service unit from the entertainment area. In the background, the dining alcove

160 The paved garden as seen from the terrace. The square of grass suggests the idea of a natural carpet in the midst of a rigorously controlled setting

sliding and fixed panels, are part of the wall that defines two sides of a paved garden. From the garden, designed in effect as an extension of the living area, one can visually appreciate the double height interior, the stair leading to the third level, the intimacy of the dining alcove, and finally, the contrast between inside and outside areas, expressed by an uncompromising use of finishing materials: white ceramic tiles on all external surfaces, painted, site-cast concrete, stone and wood in the interior.

All levels are characterized by their precise functions: the first level gives access to the house and includes the plant room. The second level, used as day area and for entertaining, has two self-contained units: the tatami room and the service unit, both served by a separate entrance. The sleeping area, reached internally by the stair in the living area and externally from the terrace, contains the master suite and two single bedrooms.

161 Looking up the open stair
that connects second to first level

162 Detail of terrace including
steps to the third level

Casa Vittoria – A Holiday Home in Pantelleria, Italy

architects:
Ll Clotet and O Tusquets
(Studio PER)
photography:
Studio PER

Midway between Sicily and Tunisia lies Pantelleria, a volcanic island protected by a preservation order as an area of outstanding natural beauty. Building permission is restricted to conversions of existing structures, with such extensions that would be either invisible from the outside or rigorously modelled on the traditional agricultural building called 'damuso'. The damuso is very similar to the simple dwellings of North Africa: square and massive, surmounted by a shallow semicircular dome and with thick dry walls of local stone.

In this project an old damuso, set well back on the terraced slope of the hill, has now become the master bedroom. A second bedroom and the bath have been added as an extension, designed and built in accordance with the simple basic volume of the original stone building. Beneath the bedrooms is the living, dining and kitchen space, partly excavated into the hillside. The particular shape of this large room is calculated to give a wide open frontage onto the sea, which can be seen

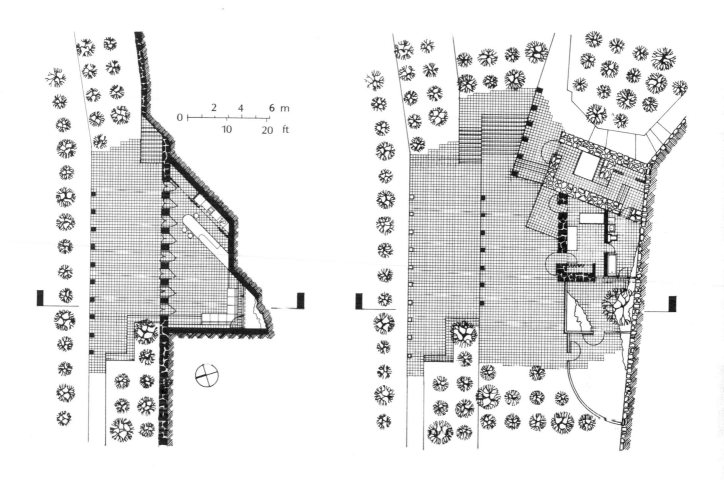

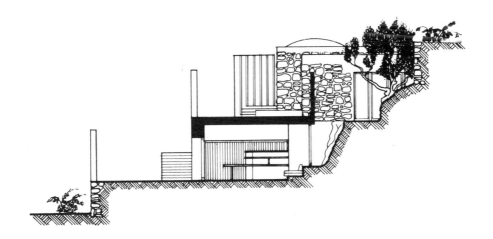

163 Looking at the house from
the hillside

164 Plans of lower and upper
levels
   1 Living space
   2 Bedroom
   3 Bathroom

165 Section

166 One of the bedrooms

through eight glass doors, and to open the house towards the hill, reached by means of a footpath at the back of the house. This double aperture provides light from two different sources and ensures cross ventilation, a fundamental necessity in the torrid summer climate.

The natural terrace formation in front of the building has been treated as a vast outdoor living space, connected by steps and sheltered from the fierce mediterranean sun by cane matting supported on concrete pillars. Seen from a distance, and in particular from the sea, these rows of pillars evoke ruins of ancient temples, and their stark simplicity agrees well with the nature of the terrain. The same tile floor was used inside and outside, and in some cases the rock outcrop was incorporated into the rooms. Accordingly, the furniture has been reduced to a simple, yet comfortable level.

167 The bathroom; note how the design of the French window allows the natural rockface inside the house

168 Another view of the upper terrace and the sea beyond

169 Looking towards the dining bar

170 Looking from the bedroom terrace towards the hillside

171 The front elevation

Temppeliaukio Church in Helsinki, Finland

architect:
Timo and Tuomo Suomalainen
photography:
Richard Einzig

This project is based on an entry that won first prize in an architectural competition announced in August 1960 and concluded five months later. A period of eight years followed, while the final plans were approved and construction methods were researched and developed. Construction began in April 1968 and the church was consecrated in September 1969.

The location, a square surrounded by apartment blocks, is not far from the centre of the city. A massive rock outcrop rising 8–13m (25–40') above street level dominated the entire open space. This rock has always been considered as an important bit of 'open country' by the inhabitants of the densely populated area surrounding the square; so it was agreed that the existing open space should be preserved.

The architects decided to set the church in a depression quarried into the rock where the street

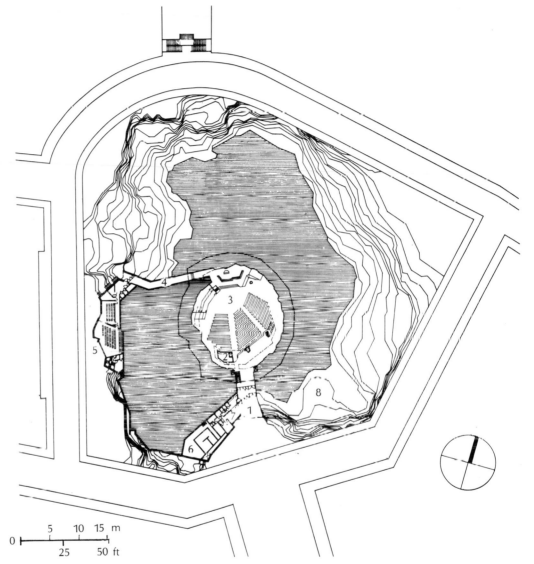

172 The main entrance to the church; note the perimeter dry wall of quarried stones held together with steel, in strong contrast with the concrete slabs set firmly into the rock, and with the clean outline of the copper-clad dome

173 Section showing the quarry line into the rock outcrop that rises gradually from the north side of Fredrikinkatu

174 Site plan
  1 Vestibule
  2 Sacristy
  3 Main church
  4 Connecting tunnel
  5 Church hall
  6 Plant room
  7 Vicar's office
  8 Rock play area

level meets that of the rock floor, at the north end of Fredrikinkatu. The plan was to follow the free form of the rock as far as possible, with auxiliary buildings located at the edge of the rock and connected to the main church by passageways. The main church was to be designed so that it could be also used as a concert hall.

The method followed for wallblasting was crevice firing, after the vertical rock slab had been firmly bolted. Average deviation from the wall line was 0.50m (1' 8"), both inwards and outwards. Drill marks were avoided as far as

possible, but not removed artificially since it was intended to let the working method show. A high degree of roughness for the interior walls was desired, both for acoustic and aesthetic reasons; the quarried stone was used in parts of the interior wall as well as in the construction of the exterior perimeter wall that shields the church from the noise of the street and of people moving around on the rock outside. This perimeter wall, and a copper dome, are practically all that can be seen from Fredrikinkatu. But on entering the main church, set below street level, one is overwhelmed by a breathtaking vision of a vast hall of granite.

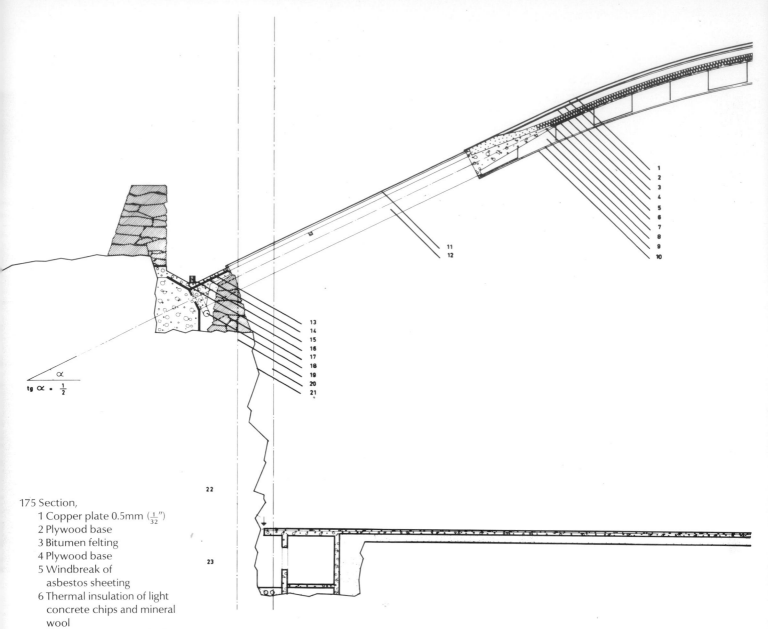

$$\text{tg } \alpha \cdot \frac{1}{2}$$

175 Section,

1 Copper plate 0.5mm ($\frac{1}{32}$")
2 Plywood base
3 Bitumen felting
4 Plywood base
5 Windbreak of asbestos sheeting
6 Thermal insulation of light concrete chips and mineral wool
7 Reinforced concrete shell
8 Acoustic baffles of asbestos sheeting
9 Wooden soffit
10 Copper cladding
11 Skylight; steel frame and insulating glass panes
12 Prefabricated reinforced concrete beam
13 Bitumen copper faced felt
14 Reinforced concrete gutter with snow-melting electrical resistors
15 Rainwater well
16 Heat insulation: mineral wool sheet
17 Quarried stone wall
18 Rainwater pipe
19 External quarry line
20 Internal quarry line
21 Rock surface
22 Gap for water drainage and air exhaust
23 Drainage pipes

A circular copper dome in the centre is surrounded by a skylight – the only source of natural light inside. According to the season, the weather, and the time of day, the hall is suffused with pale, even light or dramatically irradiated by direct sunlight that sets the pink rock aglow and projects the distorted shadows of the roof beams onto the rock surfaces.

A great deal of research was devoted to the design of the roof. A 1:25 scale model of a bearing structure, derived from a rough mathematical solution to fairly basic assumptions, was built and then loaded. Form changes, dislocations, deflection and stresses were measured at key points and the final proportions were worked out from the data thus compiled. The actual roof is a reinforced concrete shell, 70mm (2$\frac{3}{4}$") thick and 24m (79' 0") in diameter, supported on the rock by 180 slanting, precast radial beams, also of

reinforced concrete. This bearing structure is of vital importance as a design element too: the beams are of varying lengths and thus link the free form of the rock space to the mathematical shape of the dome.

The roof is the only part of the church that has been fully insulated; elsewhere the rock acts as a natural thermal insulation. The concrete shell is clad with 0.5mm ($\frac{1}{48}$") copper sheeting on a plywood base over roofing felt on plywood. The soffits of both these layers are mechanically ventilated. Below the bearing structure are sound baffles of asbestos sheet to aid sound diffusion. The soffit of the ceiling is of timber lined with a sound-penetrable cladding of 1mm ($\frac{1}{24}$") strips of copper sheeting, 20mm ($\frac{3}{4}$") wide nailed so as to give 5mm ($\frac{3}{16}$") slits between strips.

The roof beams are covered with insulating glass; the upper panes are clear glass, the lower

176 Looking from the gallery towards the main church space

are slightly tinted, laminated glass; glazing is
fixed to the steel frame with synthetic rubber
putty and brass beading.

Rain water runs into a 1.5–2m (5′–6′ 6″) wide
gutter between the lower edge of the skylight
and the perimeter stone wall. The gutter is of
reinforced concrete construction incorporating
snow-melting heating elements and lined with
copper faced bitumen felt. The water is
channelled into the main underfloor perimeter
drain inside the building; water running down
the rock face is also collected in this drain. The
entire building is connected to the city district
heating network; the main church and lobby
are heated by ducted warm air, the auxiliary
buildings by hot water radiators. Ventilation is
mechanically operated: air is blown into the
main church through inlets placed mainly in the
gallery, with air extracts running along the wall
under the floor.

Apart from the roof beams, all interior and
exterior concrete structures were cast in situ. A
set-retarding agent was added to the concrete
mix in order to avoid horizontal working joints.
The gallery is clad with 0.6mm ($\frac{1}{4}$″) copper
panelling. The main church was designed so that
direct sunlight coming through the skylight at
the front of the church falls on the altar wall
during the usual time of the morning services.
Artificial lighting is by spotlights set in the
ceiling.

The outer stone wall of the main church, the
buildings round the rock, and the concrete wall
linking them, enclose an upper courtyard more
sheltered than the rest of the rock area. The
bare character of the setting has been
successfully preserved. A heap of quarry
fragments has been left in the courtyard for the
amusement of children.

177 Detail of the gallery

178 Effects of sunlight on the altar
wall
photography: Ä Fethulla

179 One of the concrete pillars
supporting the gallery

Overpage
180 The altar wall, and part of the
ceiling. When the church is used
for concerts, the orchestra and
choir occupy the raised platform
in front of the altar. The church
will hold 940 people, but permanent seating is for 530 people
only, thus freeing a good propor-
tion of floor space for flexible
seating arrangements.

181 One from a series of six windows for the Chapel, St Antonius Hospital, Eschweiler, West Germany, 1976; 3.11 × 2.69m (10′2″ × 8′10″) Designed by Ludwig Schaffrath, West Germany

Elements of Architecture
The Window

by Patrick Reyntiens

The mysteriousness of 'connection', the connection of the outward world with the inner world – which is the central task and problem facing each man and woman, has its parallel in Architecture. The interaction of outside and inside is at the same time effected by and symbolised by the window. These areas of entry and exit, these double actioned apertures have always been the source of inspiration and metaphor in Architecture and Art since the beginning. Some would say that they are the excuse for expression irrespective of their use, and it is true that, like clocks, windows have always afforded an opportunity for an investigation into a world of idea and association far exceeding their function. Yet their function persists – not much use building a house without windows – and it looks as though the function of the window now has completely overtaken the expressive possibilities. How far this thesis is true, and how far the expressiveness of the window persists in spite of, and perhaps because of, the advent of new necessities and techniques, is the business of this article to examine.

At the outset I should say that the article is not an historical survey. I only instance history so as to demonstrate the necessity of dissolving the historical perspective (closely allied to the concept of 'progress') that has, since the 19th century, lain like a carapace on the judgement of architecture. The historical perspective which merely considers all architecture as a strict causal and serial pattern, can lead to sterility: it is based on too limited an appreciation of the possibilities of architecture. Such a rigid and short-term point of view is fairly prevalent today, and many architects create with only the achievements of the last ten years in mind. This attitude is, as Henry Ford said of history, 'bunk', and it needs debunking.

The Eye is master

From being viewed *by* the eye the window occasionally *becomes* the eye, as in Magritte or Ledoux, or the Pantheon even, where one is irradiated from above by a baleful cyclopean glare, the negative image, almost, of the eye of nemesis. The Pantheon demonstrates the window at its most oppressive and aggressive: the eye is bombarded by a pressure of light that is insupportable: irresistable by its luminous attraction, the round hole yet annihilates the attempt of the eye to escape. But in other circumstances the window can be the occasion for release: when the eye gazes from a window, as in a Renaissance engraving, and causes an imaginary come to splay from iris or retina, it is the occasion for drinking deeply into the interior of the brain a draught of the visible world. A view is proof of a window's efficiency: or is it? This really depends on the eye being able to travel outwards with the least effort; but to look out of a window with pleasure and gratification, the eye needs protection. Structural and decorative questions of soffits and mouldings, and the qualities of shade that they engender are bound to come into play as an aid to the eye in its outward motion. The embrasure of the window and the overhanging soffit on the outside of the building should be capable of acting towards the window as the eyelid and eyebrows do towards the eye in nature. The architect in the past produced a building of passion, with shadowed mouldings about the window

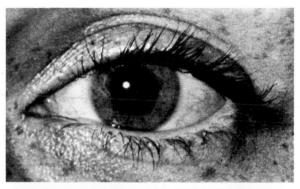

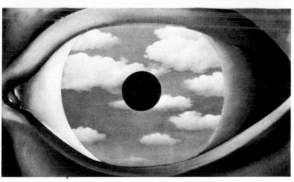

182 The Human Eye: a link between the physical and the metaphysical

183 The Pantheon, Rome (AD 120–4); the eyes symbolizing the supervision of Olympus over the universe

184 'Le Faux Miroir' by René Magritte (1928). Oil on canvas 54 × 81 (21¼″ × 31⅞″) *Collection, The Museum of Modern Art, New York*

that call to mind the Artist in Breughel's 'Kunstler und der Kenner'. If the architecture of past times recalls the 'Kunstler', the architecture of today more often than not recalls the 'Kenner' – look at the difference of the eyes of the men and the moulding, or lack of it, in the lips.

Probing a building from the outside by scrutinising the windows is a thankless task: they must have known this in times past – hence the forbidding black blocks inserted in the facades of 17th century and 18th century architectural drawings. The intense gloom of the window areas give the drawings of these buildings a curiously non-committal air, as though they were giving the spectator a blank look. The windows are well above eye level, beyond scrutiny: with their impossible sills they are designed entirely to be looked at from the outside. The 'looked at' window as such is perfected in Renaissance haughtiness. From Michelangelo and Borromini to Lutyens, the effect of stuffy grandeur is the same. Embrasures become an occasion for a symbolic language of projection and void which is primarily a language of metaphor appealing to the intelligence, and through that, perhaps, occasionally to the soul of the spectator. It is a truly 'de haut-en-bas' performance, which guarantees that the eye never is allowed to penetrate into the interior of the buildings which remain remote, hieratic, aristocratic.

This raises the question whether a window itself can be an interior-exterior passage for one's own identity and change of sensibility and mood. Man was

188 Front elevation, Coleshill, Berkshire, England, 1650–2, by Sir Roger Pratt in consultation with Inigo Jones. The windows are drawn as if detached and inexpressive: as if designed to be seen from the outside but stopping the eye from penetrating the interior

189 The twin towers of the elevation seen from the cloister, the Cathedral of Santiago de Compostela, Spain, 1738–49. Generous mouldings provide the chiaroscuro which helps to humanise architecture

certainly personified in certain buildings in the past, but this seems to be a difficult exercise to accomplish nowadays. The matière and form of architecture have alike become far less human or capable of anthropomorphism. It now seems impossible validly to construct analogous situations where the building can be equalled to the body, the body to the building. This has something to do with the disposition and quality of light and shade playing over the exterior shapes and hollows of the building; with few exceptions, the buildings of today give nothing in the way of recession and shadow content: like the 'Kenner's mouth', the meeting of surfaces and planes is too meagre, the mouldings too ungenerous.

185 'Der Kunstler und Der Kenner', by Pieter Breughel; the contrast between the 'Kunstler' (the painter) and the 'Kenner' (the connoisseur) may be paralleled by the contrast between the architecture of past ages and certain contemporary architecture: the former, rugged and creative with a face full of the richness of life; the latter, parasitic and mean in his bland features

186 Detail of window on facade, Collegio della Propaganda Fide, Rome, 1665, by Francesco Borromini. The language of classical architecture is here orchestrated into a witty, mannerist composition which does more than merely frame the window opening
Photographic Library, Courtauld Institute of Art

187 Window on the second floor, Palazzo Farnese, Rome, 1546, by Michelangelo. The window is enriched by carved mouldings and pediment which protect the view out of the window and also protect the aristocratic interior from the gaze of the commoner

133

190 IBM United Kingdom Ltd, 40 Basinghall Street, London EC2, 1965
The supposedly liberating use of curtain-walling creates a spiritual prison contrasted with the architecture of an earlier era

191 Hoover Factory, Western Avenue, Perivale, near London, 1932, by Wallis, Gilbert and Partners. German-influenced architecture in England in the 1920s and 1930s began to explore the increased use of plate glass

The effect of visual meanness in many modern buildings may well be the reflection of the supposed lack of interior resonance in the lives of the inhabitants or the people who use them daily. In this blandness, perhaps the greatest offenders are office blocks. Somehow, the more fragile-seeming a window the greater the power of physical, and ultimately spiritual, imprisonment it seems to possess. The question of 'liberation' through the mass-use of plate glass is no new subject for discussion. Frequently a new manufacturing method is invented which enables an aspiration to be fulfilled. Whether the produce is a result of the aspiration or vice versa is difficult to say. Certainly in factory buildings the idea of glass walls was well on the way to being realised before the 1914 war, as Pevsner and others never tire of reminding us: but what aspirations had they? There is a distinct acceleration in the use of plate glass after the 1914 war. Perhaps there is a metaphysical reason for this phenomenon: the cessation of war releases an immense amount of creative energy.[1] In Germany and Austria, in 1919 and beyond, so far as architecture was concerned, there was brought into being the fact of 'over-fenestration' – buildings were curtain-walled with glass, and flooded with beneficial and health-giving light. This fashionable solution to the wall-problems in much 1920's and 1930's architecture has close connection to the sun-worshipping, clothes-stripping, hiking weekenders who hopefully worked the week in such buildings only to escape into youth, health and happiness on Sundays and Saturdays. The cult of innocence seems to have been pursued on a culpable scale, and in a sense we are not through with it yet. Architecture is still gigantically committed to over-fenestration and it must be admitted that the extension of the window over most of the wall surface is a convenient solution for not facing up to certain other awkward questions such as what to do with the walls, for instance. When architecture has gained such an

[1] In 1688, following the defeat of the Turks by Austria and Poland, pent-up energy was responsible for the euphoria of the late baroque and rococo of Bavaria and Austria. From being on a permanent war footing the countries expanded into the most volatile style of architecture.

'innocence' it is all but impossible to get rid of it. The vocabulary of plane and edge and void and projection has been lost. Somehow, in the almost anti-ecological movement towards simplicity as a perfectionist goal, the humus of association and cross-references in our minds has been blown away and a bareness becomes almost a barrenness.

The freedom given by plate glass is only apparent: at best it is a severely limited freedom and in the end it may turn out to be intolerable and 'insincere'. To bring in the idea of insincerity in this context needs some explanation.[1] There seems to be an element of charade about the plate glass building. In apparently revealing all, the facade seems actually to be hiding something at the same time; we are being undersold. To reveal its true identity a company building in New York, for instance, should be emblazoned with the advertisements that are the real foundation of its prosperity and its apparently chaste inviolability. Enormous multicoloured banners of desire and satisfaction waving from the balconies (which don't exist) or floating from the crenellations (which could not exist) should decorate the buildings: then they would be a little bit nearer to telling the truth, but instead we are given the impassive fascia of the external image of business efficiency. The business building becomes once again, after 200 years, the image of the *Serene Highness*, the calm, non-personal arbiter, only this time of business, which would like the public to think that all decisions are arrived at by a process of effortlessly lucid awareness. But boardrooms are now as royal or grand ducal courts were then, racked with dissention and strife however hard the architect strives to express the exact opposite.

Telephone, tape and computer: the plate glass window protects all these activities; at the same time it extends the office itself to outward infinity, while offering this vision of infinity to those inside. The result is that nobody feels quite at home. By sheer fenestration, every New York office has now at least one giant glazed mural decoration, which happens to be, unavoidably, other offices activities. The only answer seems to be venetian blinds. They must be pulled down, otherwise those inside are in danger of over-exposure. The blindless house, like the wall-less house, becomes a prison wherein the spectator himself is nearly always the spectacle. The glass house does indeed become a 'glasshouse'[2] and the surrounding landscape, if it exists, is permanently projected onto the screens of the windows. The season's changes change the decor and the house is invaded by nature, natural functions only being screened. Is this the price of freedom? Do the blind follow the blind?

Freedom may consist in *opening* a window; because it is not enough merely to look into or out of one. The opportunity for the lightest exercise of this most innocent whim doesn't often occur in office blocks. You can't open a window there. Like the rule of 'don't touch' in museums, this is a restriction which is fundamentally against our natures. 'Don't open' and 'don't touch' are contributions towards the progressive atrophy of our senses, and hence of ourselves. The delicacy of the plate glass is totally inhibiting: most plate glass windows are fixed and only allow our vision to roam freely, never ourselves. This is lethally frustrating – not to be able to pass freely from one modality to another. Because it is in the possibility of change, from walking to standing, water to dry land, silence to speech and so on, that our true stature as humans begins to become apparent. We are varied and ever changing, and our minds harbour many different entities, each of which craves a different kind of expression. Windows should open, and we should be able to transpose easily

192 Tower Block at London Bridge, London, by T.P. Bennet, 1976
The movement of much architecture towards a rationalised simplicity is exploited by business organisations to present an often false facade of calm efficiency

193 Peter Jones Department Store, Sloane Square, London, by W Crabtree, J A Slater, A H Moberly and Sir Charles Reilly, 1935–6
Curtain-walling provides an elegant screen hiding the bustling, commercial reality of a large and successful department store

[1] *Sincerity and Authenticity* by Lionel Trilling.
[2] The 'glasshouse' is the slang term for a military prison in the British Army.

through them, either bodily or (at least) by taking a sniff of fresh air. Even the most elaborate windows of the 18th century were made to swing right open in the Summer, although at other times they might have been hermetically sealed against the cold. To take an instance, the most modest windows of the Amalienburg at Schloss Nymphenberg, Munich, were made to open – to connect the outside with the inside of the building – and made to open at whim. I can't in fact remember whether the windows in the round salon in the middle of this Dwarf Palace are French windows or not – they ought to be, and I think certainly the centre one is – but what I can remember, on that autumn day of my visit, was the shutness of the windows. Had they been open, the whole point of the freedom and delicacy of the salon's decoration would have been obvious at a glance – or at a smell, perhaps, because the silver and white and blue of the stucco would have matched the smell of lilac, or stock, or tuberoses coming in from the garden at various times of the year. The sound of the birds, too, in the trees at dusk coming in from outside would have inhabited the deeply undercut scrollwork and high relief vignettes silvered against the ceiling and encrusting the looking glasses. But 'open to the public' has other meanings now, and museum guards, government security-men and air-conditioning itself have all of them combined to make the act of opening a window an indictable offence; the violation of the 'air-conditioned nightmare'.[1]

[1] *The Air Conditioned Nightmare*, one of William Burroughs most famous works of fiction.

194 The Music Room at the Amalienburg, Schloss Nymphenburg,
Munich, Germany 1734–39
Through the open french
windows drift the scents and
sounds of nature, giving life to
their stylized representations
found in the intricate decorations
of the salon
Bildarchiv Foto, Marburg

195 The May Exhibition of Paint-
ings at the Place Dauphine, by
G St. Aubin, 1769
The etiquette of the 18th century
found physical expression in the
modern architecture of its time
*Photographic Library, Bibliothèque
Nationale, Paris*

It has been said a bit too often that architecture is frozen music. What has
not been noticed before, I think, is the correspondence between architecture
and manners. There should be a connection, I suppose, because both are
concerned with communication. Manners and architecture are in fact
inextricably bound up: the stucco rocaille of the Amalienburg is the con-
cretization of the elaborate, choreographic mode of manners of the day,
with its doffing of hats and fluttering of hands in crescendo, diminuendo,
andante and allegro. Nowadays, the very absence of formal manners, and of
formal body movement is perhaps responsible for the bleak quality of much
modern architecture. There seems to be so little interpenetration of parts or of
sensations that a connotation of humanity in architecture is difficult to find.
'Open agreements, openly arrived at' when applied to the meeting of planes, is
no basis for a subtle and human architecture. Some of the more prominent
buildings of the last two decades seem positively to hate people – they lack the
visible evidence of being involved in our lives: some, like the brittle shells of
molluscs put on display in museum cabinets, lack that 'zoomorphic' envelope
that was evident when the shell was alive. The inhumanity of that architecture
which seems connected to manufacture and commerce, lies in the neglect of
just those factors that constitute this 'zoomorphic envelope': for example
people, artefacts, gardens, smells, water, noise (the right sort of noise); to say
nothing of sudden shifts of scale, direction and level. All these extra and vital

.196 Clapboard terrace-housing, Pleasant Hill, Kentucky, USA, early 19th century.
The very human architecture of the exclusive, ideal world of the Shakers, totally divorced from the commercial life of a vast and powerful nation.

197 View through a window, Pleasant Hill, Kentucky, USA.
The lines of this gothic Shaker window reflect the tracery of the trees beyond, framing and expressing a particular view of nature in relation to man

factors come originally from the architect's being the servant of clients who really knew what the business of living was about. The 'getting back to essentials' of the 1920's, particularly of the Bauhaus, in this respect went too far. In most cases the 'essentials' happened not to be the same as the 'vitalising' element. Can one 'get back to essentials' in that sense? I think not. The 'fundamental' appealed to is too much a figment of the imagination, and too pragmatically chosen to hold any conviction. Of course the attractions of a *tabula rasa* have perhaps always been with us; it is not new; from the Cistercians to the Shakers there have always been movements of renewal and self-denial and clean uncluttered rebuilding towards a better, more ideal world. I suppose we all aspire to an 'ideal world' but this aspiration can take either of two forms: aspiration by *inclusion* or *exclusion*. The Bauhaus like the Cistercians, opted for exclusion and it became undoubtedly one of the prime examples of the principles of the Exclusive Brethren applied to an art and architecture situation: all this in the name of humanity. The Bauhaus was an appeal to a kind of mechanistic primitivity: the windows, or rather the wall, (for fenestration and wall are one) demonstrate this by their ruthless integrity.

Real primitive living, that is living stripped to its most basic, is not unlike the world of trench and dugout that perhaps the Brave New World of Bauhaus was intent on saving humanity from. Nothing could go further in this 'trench warfare' than the caves of Cappadocian cenobites. In these geological cones of silence, the windows give the impression of being purely accidental – mere perforations that appear haphazardly as a result of burrowings from within. Except for the entrance-hole in each cone, there is scarcely any reason for the windows to appear at all, so concerned with the extremes of interiority were the monks. Like insects in root-artichokes, the makers of the windows would have been far happier, one feels, if their activities had never come to light. It must have been quite a surprise for each solitary inhabitant to discover at the chance flake-off, or fall-out of the side of a chamber that the neighbours were at it as well. An irreparable mistake, it seems, this haphazard self-exposure of holiness and solitude: and no 'ancient lights'. The resultant windows were ever open – couldn't be shut – and this perpetual breath of fresh air probably saved the monks from too close and serious an introspection. . . .

Consciousness of another sort, having nothing to do with open windows and fresh air, is implicit in the ideals of religious architecture. In connection with religious architecture, it is interesting to note that the relationship between the contemplative faculty and the amount of light falling on the eye has never, up to now, been properly investigated.

198 West facade of the Cistercian Monastery at Pontigny, France, 12th century
A much earlier exclusive community, founded in the 11th century as a reaction against the extravagance of the Benedictine system, the Cistercians built stately, severe buildings which are a perfect shelter for their simple life, stripped of all inessentials
Photographic Library, Caisse Nationale © *Arch. Phot. Paris/S.P.A.D.E.M.*

199 Caves of Cappadocian cenobites, Turkey
Windows appear to be irrelevant in these caves for introspective thought. The monks needed no contact with life outside in their retreat from everything worldly

The vast majority of religious buildings have been heavily sedated on the window plane. This is not due to inefficiency of fenestration in large buildings, but to a change in psychological awareness that occurs in an interior of relative gloom. The faculties of reminiscence and contemplation seem to expand, just as they recede almost to nothing in a brightly lit interior. The manipulation of psychological possibilities in buildings should be the result of deliberate calculation, and to a large degree it does depend on the actual amount of light allowed into the interior. Now, space, in the physical sense, is not of the essence when dealing with psychological factors. Very small buildings can suggest enormous vistas of ideas and possibilities; one can instance in this respect the Cabinet in the Ducal Palace at Urbino or the small dining-room in the Sir John Soan Museum in Lincoln's Inn Fields, London. These master-pieces defy the criterion of size alone, and create enormous psychic space. Psychic space is the result of the projection of our sensibilities into other dimensions of life, or of consciousness: it is essentially the result of a psycho-logical enlargement depending on architectural ingenuity and light, and on associations, memorabilia and thematic material. One could say there is an element of the dramatic in it too, and would almost be forced to include *Faust* or the *Ring* cycle within the concept of psychic space.

At no time was the idea of psychic space understood better than in the Middle Ages. The ideas behind the employment of stained glass in the Abbey of St Denis, for instance, were to construct a model of paradise on earth, for the faithful to contemplate in a truly platonic way; St Denis was designed to lead the spectator on from 'fair forms' to 'fair notions'. Nor was Suger concerned only with re-creating paradise in the sanctuary, but in constructing a microcosm of the universe by means of the building of the church. The vast expanses of colour on the window plane in the medieval cathedral reinforced this macro-microcosmic intention. The cathedral became a visual data-bank of all that was vital in the conscious business-transaction of saving one's own soul. The memorable images and themes, histories and hagiographies, were the 'services' for the mind and soul; just as today electricity, water, heat, and communication are the 'services' in a building which are considered essential for present day convenience.

In the process of being a philosophic model of reality, as it was understood in the Middle Ages, the cathedral became the embodiment of that central idea of duality of body and soul, which haunted those ages of defective medicine and diseased physique. The stone architecture of the building stands as a fit analogy to the human body.[1] The light streaming in from the historiated windows becomes analogous to the spiritual light irradiating the soul; matter and spirit interpenetrate. On a cloudy and windy day in York or Chartres or Bourges, standing in the nave, one feels that the whole cathedral breathes – the shadows of the clouds, as they pass darkening the church, being the outgoing exhalation and the sun's return becoming the inspiring breath. One is conscious of being inside a living organism that is gently kinetic on the vastest scale – ever moving yet ever the same. One interesting instance of the quality of light coming through windows, which appears to be wildly inappropriate, is that of the Sainte Chapelle. At first glance the stained glass seems far too heavy in character for the fragility of the architecture. They don't seem to fit together. But then one realises that the chapel is really a unique coup-de-théatre, not a parish church, and the subdued light produces an atmosphere of magical unreality that surrounds the beholder in a suspension of disbelief.

[1] A theme that is more explicit in Renaissance imagery perhaps. Cf. Andreas Vesalius's book of anatomy *De Humani Corporis Fabrica* with its overtones of the idea of the human body being architecture, and John Donne referring to his ribs as the 'rafters' of his body.

200 La Sainte Chapelle, Paris, looking east, built by Pierre de Montreuil (1243–8)
Vast expanses of stained glass set in a delicate gothic frame form a model of heaven on earth which, in itself, is a microcosm of the universe. The glass appears too heavy and yet the subdued light produces an aura of reverence

201 Three windows from a set of
nave windows in St Joseph's
Church, Aachen, West Germany,
by Ludwig Schaffrath, 1970–72.
The art of stained glass is very
much alive in West Germany
and, using traditional materials,
often in traditional buildings as in
this case, several artists are ex-
perimenting with this revitalised
means of expression. Ludwig
Schaffrath excels in creating windows that are always in harmony
with their architectural setting

202 The Chapel of the Holy
Shroud, Turin Cathedral, Italy, by
Guarino Guarini, 1667–90.
Arches spring up heavenwards to
support the circle of the dome
where light floods into the interior through more arched
openings. Here again, light and
architecture combine to create
an ideal setting for the rites con-
ducted below, or simply to inspire private devotion

True, the atmosphere of the cathedral has changed in the course of the last five
hundred years. By architectural change, accretion and depletion, and a
reordering of liturgy, the effect of the medieval church must now be very
remote – possibly only in the Russian Orthodox Church could we experience
some of the religious atmosphere of medieval Europe. Stained glass windows
could not open, that is true, but their iconography liberated the soul even if
their being permanently shut suffocated the lungs. And suffocated the lungs
certainly were. The 'Botafumero' used at Santiago de Compostela, for instance,
was a six-foot silver censer swung from transept to transept through a sixty-
foot arc, precisely to deal with the situation of not being able to open windows,
the incense being a prophylactic against the sweat and feet of the pilgrims
packed tightly overnight into the cathedral. . . .

There is an element, in medieval art, of synaesthesia, a cross-referencing of the
senses. This is not simply making use of the whole gamut of the senses –
though that certainly might come into it – so much as melding the different
stimuli into a coherent whole, where no one part predominates over another.

It leads one to the thought that, perhaps, those who are tone deaf and have no nose for incense cannot truly understand the ultimate dimension of awareness inherent in the stained glass windows of the middle ages.

Two major instances of synaesthetic art in architecture immediately come to mind: both are by Guarini, one of the most original and profound architects of all time. His two structures of the Chapel of the Holy Shroud, Turin, and the Church of St Lawrence are perhaps the most eclectic buildings ever conceived; baroque, saracenic, gothic and renaissance elements contributing to a whole which aspires to a mystical penetration and presentation of form *beyond* the aspirations of architecture. They are both of unique significance. Note for example the fenestration in the domes of these two buildings: there is a certain truth in the conviction that, to be properly seen, these churches ought to be prayed in before eight in the morning and after six in the evening. Only then will the horizontal light coming through the windows give the impression of an expansion of the interior and a volatization of the dome structure, towards a vision which is beyond architecture; an impression reinforced by the act of praying whilst kneeling over a long time period. Perhaps this will be a near-to-impossibility for some – but it is well worth trying. A similar instance of the dissolution of architecture through light into vision, though in a far more blatant way, is the Transparente, by Narciso Tomé, in Toledo Cathedral; the effect of light coming through the skylight above aspires to a mystical vision; and it succeeds, if only in contrast to the sobriety of the 13th century ambulatory. Again, I believe that the Transparente was designed to be seen pretty early in the morning, when the sun is horizontal and the skylight catches the full glare of the early rays which turn and stream downwards, thus literally blinding the spectator with glory. It may well have only been appreciated by the charwomen of Toledo coming in to the

203 The 'Transparente', Toledo Cathedral, Spain, by Narciso Tomé; completed in 1732. Tomé obtained the source of light by removing the masonry between the ribs of half the original Gothic vault.

Cathedral for six o'clock mass. Gaudí, in his Sagrada Familia Church at Barcelona, (where the fenestration is reasonably conventional in a neo-gothic way) and in his Capilla Guëll (which is in *no way* conventional), strives to produce an effect which is overall more than the sum total of the architectural means employed.[1]

In the medieval cathedral the glass of the windows is par excellence the interpretative medium, whereas in Gaudí's work the sculpture and decoration are. Both Gaudí and the medieval mason imply a transcendentalism that is today quite out of fashion.[2] However eccentric Gaudí seems to have been at the time in his aesthetic and religious aims, the building methods he improvised were not exclusively related, or even necessarily appropriate, to the expression of religious themes.

The style known as 'Art Nouveau', which was truly international, was concerned as never before with the synthesising of different sensations, above all through the use of different materials. All the inventions of the 19th century building industry were pressed into use, particularly combinations of glass, metal, wood and brick. Construction, applied art and craft weld together to produce an effect of convincing, though slightly hysterical opulence, and even the nuts and bolts of the construction contribute a kind of regular embossment of design in counterpoint to the sinuous, 'copied direct from nature' quality of the applied art. The work of Montañer and Jujol in Spain, Guimard and Majorelle in France and Van der Velde and Horta in the Low Countries all have this synaesthetic quality. The Art Nouveau was the penultimate age of craftsmanship in art applied to buildings, the Style Déco being the last; but the Style Déco was a mere stylistic coda before the financial crashes of the late 1920's succeeded in putting everyone's mentality onto a war footing.

204 The Towers of the Sagrada Familia, Barcelona, Spain, by Antoni Gaudí, 1903–26.
These towers, seen against the background of the earlier pinnacles of the presbytery, are an example of architecture at its most plastic. Sculptural qualities have taken over so that decoration and essential structure cannot be separated

[1] Gaudí appreciated the great Baroque alterpieces and set pieces of 17th and 18th century Spain and had the self confidence born of the unbroken continuity and tradition in 19th century Spain to refurbish completely the chancel of the 13th century cathedral in Palma de Mallorca in a high Art Nouveau style.

[2] Perhaps a law could be formulated that the more lofty the ideal in religion and politics the more synaesthetic solutions seem appropriate . . . (that is taking it for granted that churchmen and politicians are interested in art and architecture). This would explain Palace as well as Cathedral. It might be objected that the Victorian pub is a prime example of the opposite, synaesthesia being bound up with low life. As a counter to that it should be noted that Victorian pubs are to be seen in polarity to the Victorian High Church Movement. Both phenomena stem from the same situation, namely the threadbare paucity of working people's lives at that time, and a determination to effect some sort of change in them through art, entertainment and devotion.

Though as eccentric as Gaudí, but in another direction, the two masterpieces
of Rudolph Steiner at Dornach, near Basel, should not be forgotten. I refer to
the Goetheanum I and II (the first being made of wood was burnt down, to be
instantly replaced by the second in concrete). Although Steiner did not live to
see the completion of the second Goetheanum, half temple, half theatre, it is
certain that it follows the lines he had conceived and intended. Whether the
windows, which are odd, yet reassuring, shapes, were filled with stained glass
exactly as he intended is not so certain. Seen from the inside each bay has a
window of a different hue so that the interior is flooded with bands of light
whose colour surely has a close reference to Rudolph Steiner's doctrines concerning the interpenetration of spirit and matter. I find the colour too violent
and the iconography confusing, but that does not detract from the scale of
Steiner's achievement. The presence of the audience in the Goetheanum
inclines to worship rather than to entertainment and the Goethaenum differs
completely from a festival theatre such as that conceived for Bayreuth
by Richard Wagner, in that its purpose is 'real' rather than artistic or allegorical.
Stylistically the Goetheanum can be defined as Art Nouveau built at precisely
the time when others were building churches, such as the Antonius Kirche
in nearby Basel, which were midway between Style Déco and Bauhaus.
The outer form of the Goetheanum owes its success to the formidable skill of
the shuttering which held the concrete in place whilst it was setting, and which
has, curiously enough, only the Maginot line, the efforts of the Todt
organisation and Le Corbusier as progeny.

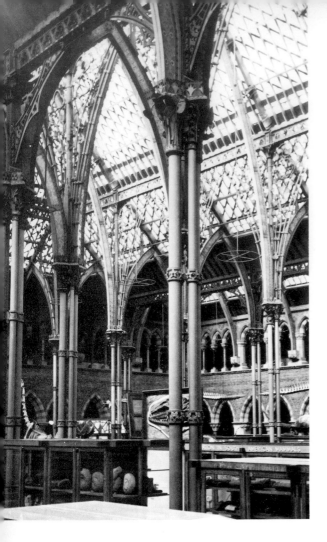

In all the architectural examples I have been viewing, from Guarini to Steiner, new visions seem to call for new techniques. This is the right way round. By themselves new techniques never call forth new visions; there are periods in history, however, when the two interpenetrate in a very interesting way. For instance, the cheapness of fuel, in the form of coal, enabled not only railways but greenhouses to run efficiently for the first time. There is a connection between the mass-entertainment of day-trippers to the Great Exhibition (itself a giant conservatory) and the raising of millions of conservatory pot plants, which were carpet-bedded in esplanades of searing colour that echoed, outside the exhibition hall, the garish designs of the Brussels broadloom carpets inside. Glass, coal, flowers, locomotives and carpets combine to effect a new, if degenerate, sensibility. In this respect Paxton's conservatory was an innovation that is yet to be fully played out; after all, Buckminster Fuller is still fascinated by the idea of glass domes.

From our point of view, the glass hangars of the termini, themselves the whelps of the Great Exhibition, present the spectator with something that is unexpected and indigestible. There is no interior or exterior to adduce in the experience of the terminus. Hitherto, light coming into a building had been clearly identified as coming through windows; but what is the reaction when the very wall itself is a window – not only the wall but the roof; and, as in the case of the department store Samaritaine in Paris, the floors are glass as well.[1] The result is to make the spectator feel slightly encephalitic; the only and prompt solution to this is to board the train and leave the platform. The age of Kinetics has dawned: henceforth the Kinetic element becomes an integral factor in architecture, adding to commodity, stability and delight. Engineering in the 19th century assumes a romance denied to poetry. Speed is enlightenment and enlightenment may be sampled in the 'Galerie aux Machines', themselves made for speed. 'Whirr whirr all by wheels! Whizz whizz all by steam'.[2] This kinetic myth, applied to architecture, takes over too much and, in the end, leads to the excessive horizontal lines in extra-urban architecture of the 1920's and 1930's, the lines being *progressive*, that is, implying speed in transit from one point to another. When this kind of architecture, which was designed to be appreciated from a car going at 30–40 miles an hour, is brought into the centres of small towns the resultant destruction is only too evident.

The visionary architecture which was conceived, but largely abandoned unfulfilled, in Germany and Austria in the 1920's was based on the achievements of 19th century technology; spiritually however it owes a lot to the fascination for the intelligentsia of Europe of the philosophies of the East and of Spiritualism, which gained such a hold on the imagination in the late 19th and early 20th century and spread far through France (cf. Schuré; les Grands Initiés) and Russia, as well as Austria and Germany. To express such hopes and transcendental dreams of perfection it was necessary to employ light, directional light, for the first time as an expressive medium in architecture. This explains the appearance of projected lights which occur in the designs of Finsterling, Taut, Gaudí and others. The intention was to extend the lines of the building outward, into the night sky, giving a phosphorescent glow of reassurance and hope. The effect would have been, possibly, like that of moveable antennae of insects or the articulated spines of the sea urchin. These somewhat bizarre aspirations were eventually thwarted by the spirit of

[1] The Samaritaine was the first building entirely constructed of square modules; ceilings, walls, floors were all glass dalles let into steel frames. This is not visible today owing to carpeting and internal walls.

[2] The Pasha's esteem of Britain as expressed in Alexander Kinglake's *Eothen*.

208 University Museum, Parks Road, Oxford, England, by Sir Thomas Deane, Son and Woodward of Dublin, 1855–60.
The innovative Victorian architecture of iron and glass, popularized by Paxton's Crystal Palace of 1851, inspired architects and engineers of the age with a new interpretation of enclosure

209 Iron and glass roof, Paddington Railway Station, London, 1850, by Isambard Kingdom Brunel.
The railway stations of the Victorian age provide an example of architectural anomaly: the roof is now also a window

210 UNESCO House, Paris, 1962.
The functions of the wall and window have been physically separated: an excessive area of glass which forms the boundary of the interior has to be shielded from the sun by a permanent brise-soleil
Photographic Library, UNESCO

Bauhaus rationalism in the 1930's and were caricatured by the events of the 1939–40 war, when moving pencilled lights probing the sky had quite other connotations.

The employment of glass revetment of buildings in a continuous skin is again a prolongation and refinement of 19th century technological innovations, but the technical possibilities governing a work of art do not explain its spiritual motivation, and the employment of large expanses of plate glass which by the 1920's had become possible through technological research was really validated by certain medical theories of the time involving uncritical self-exposure to the sun. Had a style of architecture, whose main constituents would have been plate glass and projected light ever truly come to maturity, the excess of light in the interiors of buildings would have been intolerable. As it is, a tendency to over-fenestrate persists to this day, and it is very difficult to make out a coherent case for buildings which have to have permanent brise-soleils built into their facades. Too much light can be as destructive as too little: the masterpieces of modern architecture are those where the balance of structure and light creates both real and psychological interior spaces. Perhaps the Gumma Prefectural Museum of Modern Art in Takasaki, by Arata Isozaki, is an example of excellence of design and quality of building materials combining to produce such a balance.

211 The entrance hall of the
Gumma Prefectural Museum of
Modern Art in Takasaki, Japan, by
Arata Isozaki, 1974.
Light coming from the vast
glazed areas combines successfully with the reflective interior
surfaces to counteract the rigidity
of the modular concept

The recovery of Germany since 1945 has been the greatest political and
economic achievement in the last thirty years. A material recovery is one
thing, certainly, but the spiritual and aesthetic motivation of the new buildings
of Germany should be carefully considered. Perhaps since the early 18th
century there have been few chances to rebuild and experiment on such a
wide scale in a new style of architecture and expression, over Western
Germany, as was given at the close of the last war. The vast rebuilding
programme of churches, and of institutes of social welfare and learning
connected to the Church, gave the stained glass artists of Germany an
unparallelled opportunity to experiment in their medium. Most of the
significant achievements of German glass are in lead calmes: very few are in

212 The interior of the Parish
Church of St George, Bleibach,
near Frieburg, West Germany,
showing part of a series of
windows by Jochem Poensgen.
The artist achieves a striking
effect using economical means of
colour and materials

213 'Orange', 49 × 39 (1'7¼" ×
1'3¼") by Johan Thorn Prikker,
1931.
This panel, made shortly before
the artist's death in 1932, is a
remarkable example of Thorn
Prikker's abstract designs, and
anticipates much post-war work

214 One of two stained glass
windows, 1.22mm × 41 (' × 1'4")
designed by Johannes Schreiter
1975, and made at the Derix
Studio, Wiesbaden, West
Germany.
These windows are based on a
series made for St Lubentius

Church, Dietkirchen, West
Germany. They demonstrate the
artist's 'free' style in the use of
lead, considered as expressive as
glass and light

new techniques such as concrete or epoxy resin. Yet this adherence to old techniques of making stained glass windows was precisely the reason for the expansion of vision and new ideas. Artists of the calibre of Johannes Schreiter, Ludwig Schaffrath, and George Meistermann, to name only three masters, could not have produced the vast output they have had they not relied on the well-tried technique and medium. What is their achievement? First, the setting. True to the German genius of creating art that is complementary to building (an attitude that goes back through history from the Rococo to the Romanesque) the stained glass of the last thirty years in Germany never consciously fights against the architectural setting. More often than not the setting is in modern architecture of a fair, but not outstanding, quality, and the expressiveness of the interior does depend for effect to a large extent on the quality of the glass in the windows. Most of this is either opalescent or opaque and very little is highly coloured. Sometimes, exceptionally, the colour scheme is confined to one dominant colour; but more often only a smattering of colour runs through a whole range of windows. The idiom in any case is invariably non-figurative. It is worthwhile realising the subconscious reasons for this. First, it is admitted freely by the artists that they wish to keep the pressures of modern existence at bay in the interiors they create with their stained glass. In this, Germany now is not perhaps different from the Gothic world of 400 years ago; but the means of effecting this separation is reversed. In Gothic times, with the rarity of colour, churches were heightened with an expressiveness which was way above the possibilities available to more mundane buildings; the outside world was very drab, the churches bright and gay. The reverse is true in Germany now; with mass advertising, the connotation attached to large areas of colour is too reminiscent of commercial brainwashing: the crass ineptitude of coloured posters, and the indiscriminate use of colour in public, have made the employment of colour in the public arts extremely suspect. The German achievement has created cells of contemplation away from the pressurised existence of the outside world.

The question of non-figuration is important. Perhaps quite inconsciously Germany has acquiesced in an abstract, grey, opalescent art form as a means of expressing its longing for a certain collective amnesia. One's eyes are bandaged, and the light is only allowed in on the strictest laid-down terms. It is difficult to see where the present enormous achievement of German glass will lead to, from a thematic or stylistic point of view, because the least hint of figurative art leads to a revamping of the Gothic idiom; and this is quite unacceptable.

The German achievement in leaded glass has avoided solutions involving plate glass. This could indicate an opposition to the vision that plate glass seems to express – a vision of immediacy, clarity, shallowness and utility – the other vision of modern German society, perhaps, or for that matter a vision of any other international modern society. This is to an extent true: certainly the employment of plate glass in works of art is rare, and when it is employed gives an effect of frigid exclusivity. One only has to instance the works of Larry Bell, for example. Delicate and fastidious as they are, the effect is one on the spectator of the work of art hating the public. Problems concerning the employment of plate glass in works of art have yet to be resolved; but these problems are not unconnected to the still unresolved reconciliation of the exterior of a building with its interior.

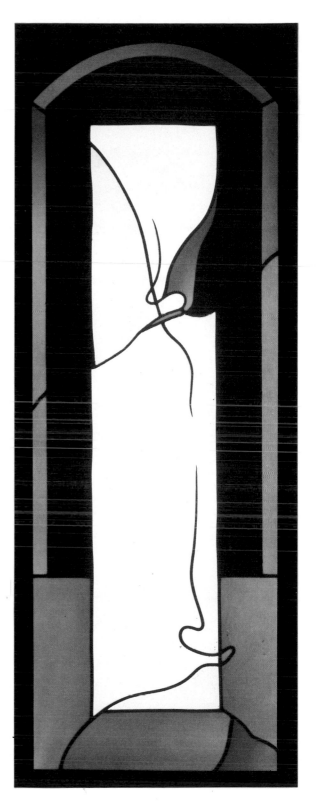

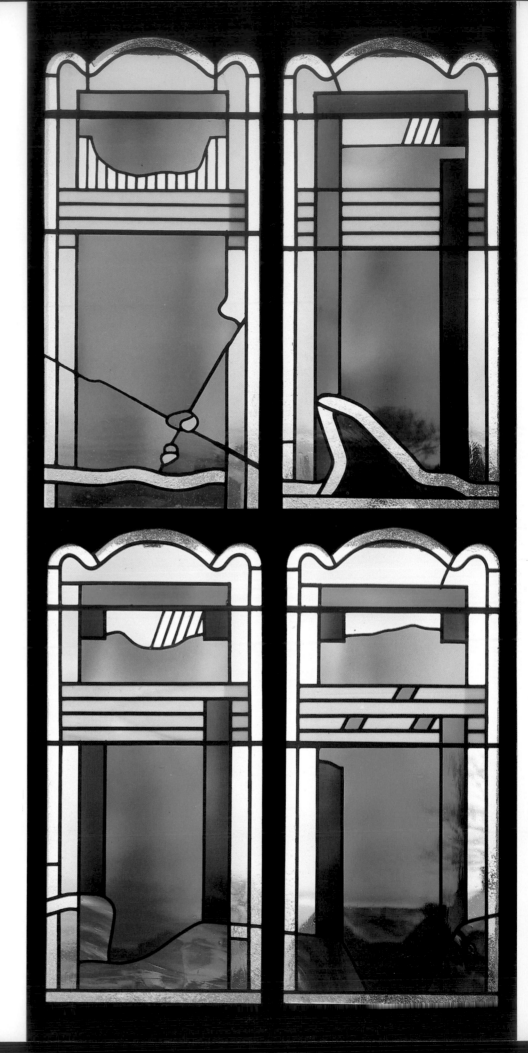

215 Windows at Longridge Parish
Church, England, by Brian Clarke,
1975.
Brian Clarke (borh 1953) was the
first British designer of stained
glass to travel extensively in
Germany in 1974 and to assim-
ilate in his work the influence of
contemporary German stained
glass. The series of ten two-light
windows as Longridge, Lancashire, are inspired by the art of
sequential Japanese screen
painting

216 Panel with a Yellow
Background, 1.52m × 1.52m
(5' × 5'), by Dick Weiss, 1976.
This artist uses traditional techniques in a fresh, uninhibited
manner; this panel expresses his
love for optical effects and for the
properties of simple glass
photography: John Frey

153

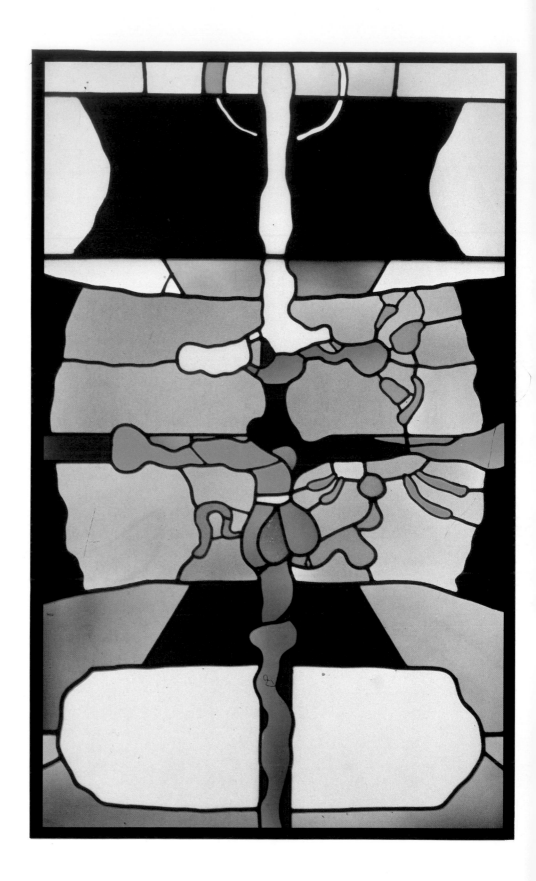

217 'The Cross', 1.53 × 93 (5' × 3'), by Patrick Reyntiens, 1966. This panel is particularly interesting in relation to contemporary German work of the mid-1960s. Made for an exhibition of the artist's work at the Building Centre, London, 'The Cross' is now in the collection of the Victoria & Albert Museum, London

Trends in Furnishing and in the Decorative Arts

218 Armchair; hand-made frame using traditional Japanese jointing methods; solid cedar wood; plastic foam seat and back, wool upholstery
Designed by Kenji Fujimura, and made in the designer's workshop, Japan

219 Two Sculptures, 1977; hand-built stoneware with chamotte glaze; 11.5 × 17 (5″ × 7″) and 22.5 × 27.5 (9″ × 11″)
Made by Inger Thing, Denmark

220 'Accordion Gesture', hanging,
1975; using cotton and hard
wools in plain colours, Warren
Seelig weaves simple lengths of
cloth. He then folds the fabric in
ways suggested by its physical
properties and inserts pieces of
vinyl to make the cloth rigid;
cotton double cloth, vinyl plastic
skeleton; white, black and red;
1.93 × 1.02 × 4
(6′ × 4″ × 3 × 4″ × 2″)
Designed and made by Warren
Seelig, USA *Courtesy of the
Hadler Galleries, New York*

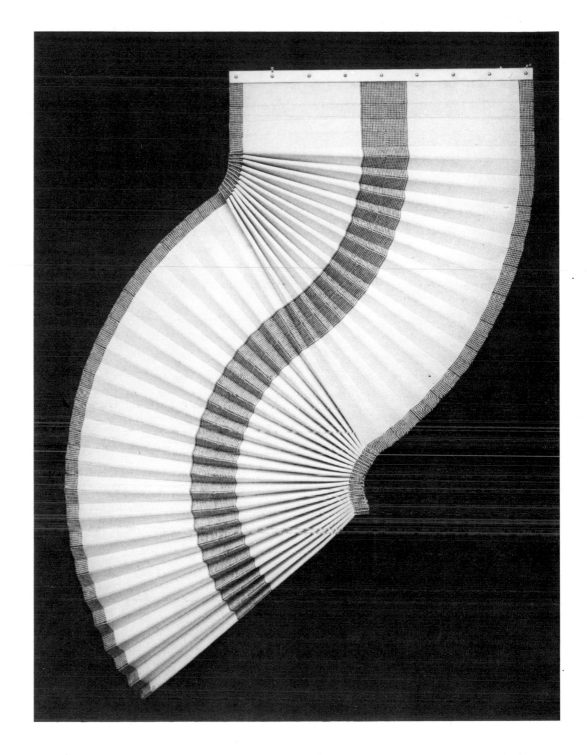

222 'Anfibio' sofa-bed; the straps, held together by heavy duty press-studs, undo to form a bed base; steel frame in polyurethane foam of various density, wrapped in dacron quilting; leather or woven upholstery; the model is produced in three sized measuring 65 × 98 × 1.10, 1.84 or 2.40m (2'2" × 3'3" × 3'7", 6' or 7'10") when folded

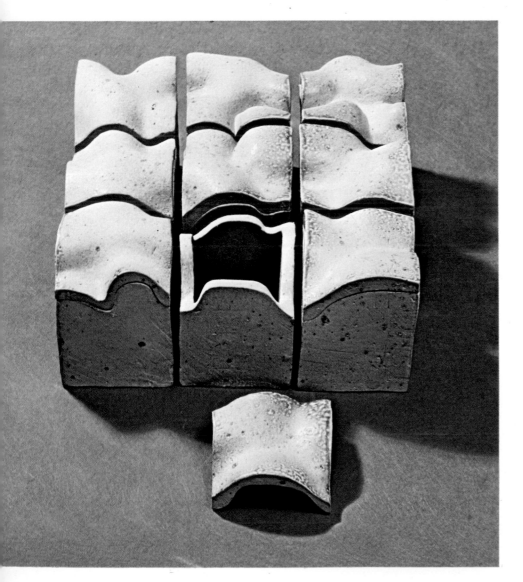

221 Nine 'landscape' boxes; salt glaze stoneware, hand-built; 35 × 35 × 12 (13¾" × 13¾" × 4¾") Made by Bente Hansen, Denmark

223 'Diletto' sofa-bed; by pushing
the backrest towards the seat a
locking mechanism is released
and the sofa converts into a
double bed; the covering unzips
to reveal the mattress and
doubles as a quilt; polyurethane
foam on steel frame;
80 × 100 × 2.35m
(2′7″ × 3′3″ × 7′8″) when locked
Both designed by Alessandro
Becchi for Giovannetti, Italy

224 Jug; coiled stoneware, salt
glaze; 20 (4¾″) high
Made by Bente Hansen Denmark

226 Three small boxes of various
hardwoods, turned on a lathe;
7.5 × 12.5 (3″ × 5″)
The patterns on the lids are cut
with engraving tools by means of
an attachment to the lathe,
which is in effect a swinging jig
controlling the movement of the
gravers. A rough blank for the
box and lid is turned first of all
and dried; then the pattern is cut
on the lid blank and afterwards
the box is finished by the normal
process of turning. The method
for doing this, and the appliance
for it, were developed by the artist
in recent years
Made by David Pye, England

225 Desk Chair; the design is inspired by a traditional type of
ship captain's chair, and the back
is formed from twelve separate
pieces cut in the solid; mahogany
veneered with yew and inlaid
with ebony; 75 × 60 (2′6″ × 2′)
Designed and made by Rupert
Williamson, England

227 Bowl, 1976; glazed stoneware, brown inside, outside white
with blue-green decoration;
15 × 18 (6″ × 7″)
Made by Richard Kjaergard,
Denmark

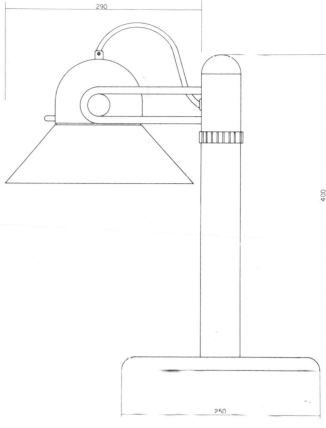

228 Adjustable reading lamp: the top section of the lamp can swivel through 360 degrees and the shade itself can be adjusted; metal lacquered maroon or dark green; 40 (15") high
Designed by Gae Aulenti for Stilnovo, Italy

229 Writing table; Laminated hardwood, carved, with inlaid top
Designed by Wendell Castle and made in limited editions in the Wendell Castle Workshop, USA

230 'Mondial', a range of arm-
chairs and settees; the basic
shape of the backrest is common
to all versions of this model and
reflects the designer's concern for
the production of a large range of
comfortable models that require
a minimal number of tubular
metal frames, thus simplifying the
manufacturing process

231 Full range of the 'Mondial'
model

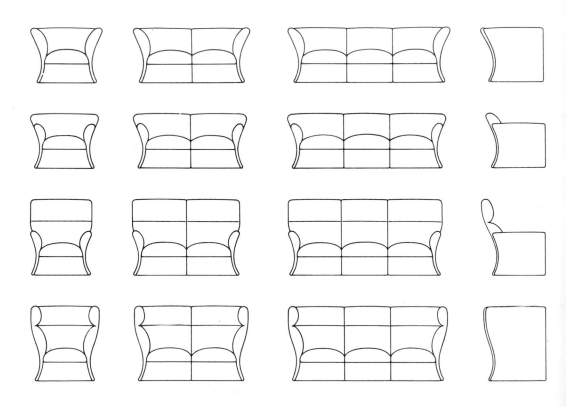

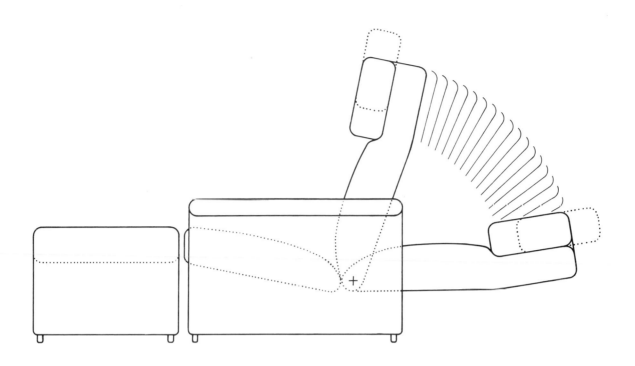

232 'Flexus', multi-adjustable
chair designed by using the techniques of car-seat manufacture.
Such seats have long been the
subject of ergonomic research
into the need to provide seating
that is comfortable over long
periods of time. The chair incorporates a reclining mechanism
similar to that used in car seats.
This offers twenty-two different
seating angles adjustable through
sixty-six degrees at three degrees
intervals. The adjustment is operated through a simple lever
system fitted below the right arm.
The chair also has a built-in head
rest, which again is adjustable to
suit individual requirements. High
quality upholstery on a well
cushioned steel frame virtually
guarantees a comfort that can be
specially adjusted to suit the user.
Both the 'Mondial' and the
'Flexus' range are produced by
L C P Trim Ltd, England

233 'Dogalina', cylindrical vases with a narrow rim, and 'Contarina' vases and bowl; mould-blown clear crystal glass with murrina decoration in blue, green or red with matching rim; bowl 14 × 28 (6″ × 11″), vases 18, 27, 30, 36 and 40 (7″, 11″, 12″, 14″, 16″) high
Designed by Luciano Vistosi for Vetreria Vistosi, Italy

234 'Badger', a miniature land-scape supported by a silver stand at the back; 5.5 × 6.5 (2⅛″ × 2½″)

235 'Train' pendant; 5 × 2¼ (2″ × ¾″)
These pieces are silver reliefs with enamel inlays, a technique developed from the traditional champ-levé method
Made by Anthony Hawksley, England

236 'The Four Seasons' bowls;
clear sodaglass recycled by the
artists from wine bottles, cased
decoration of commercial
coloured glass; 13.5 (5") high
Made by Finn Lynggaard,
Denmark

237 Container, 1977; shaped as
though made of leather, decor-
ated with imitation zip fasteners;
stoneware with glazed interior;
37 × 11 × 23 (14" × 4" × 9")
Made by Karen Bennicke,
Denmark

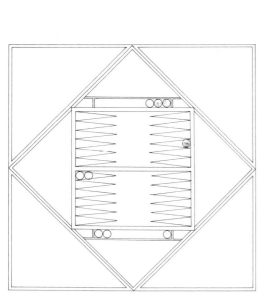

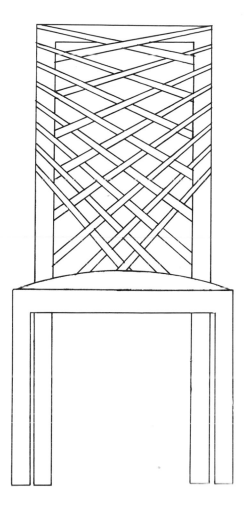

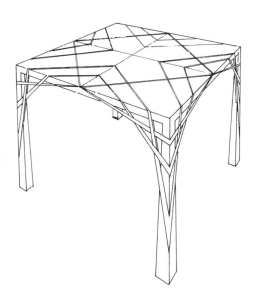

238 Games Table and Chairs; by means of a rose in the centre of the table, four flaps fold back to reveal the games inside; the table top is 2.5 (1″) thick at the edge, increasing to 7.5 (3″) in the centre to contain the games. The design of the frame is structural as well as decorative: the diagonal members help to brace the table then continue into the table top as inlaid decoration. The chairs also make use of diagonal members in their delicate backs, every section being carved out of solid wood and assembled with secret joints, one of the characteristics of this artist's work.

English maple inlaid with myrtle, table top veneered with birdseye maple, centre rose of silver and mother-of-pearl; interior lined with synthetic suede which is also used to cover the chair seats; all wood is finished with high gloss polyester varnish; table 1 × 1m × 74 (3′3″ × 3′3″ × 2′5″)
Designed and made by Rupert Williamson, England

The furniture pieces illustrated here are the product of the inter-action between their designer, Gijs Bakker, and the Dutch furniture company, Castelijn. Formerly known for his jewelry, Gijs has moved from a traditional craft base to work alongside industry. When designing he keeps the manufacturing process in mind. He believes that the pro-ducer and the consumer have been distanced by the increas-ing sophistication of the tech-nology used in manufacture. The designer is able to bridge this gap and to maintain his freedom he should remain independent. His designs are first drawn up on paper at home and a scale-model made. This model then becomes the basis of discussion between himself and the manufacturer and they work closely together to produce a prototype. Gijs Bakker does not wish to humanise tech-nology; indeed he believes this to be impossible. To him, tech-nology is a tool which increases the means of expression

240 'Webbing Chairs', 1978; a basic design which has been adapted to produce an armchair, a dining room chair, a bar stool and a baby chair; ash frame with a natural, white or black finish, seat woven from webbing origin-ally produced for safety-belts in cars

239 'Torsion Chair', 1973/77; a prototype design, not yet in pro-duction; laminated bentwood frame, with woven cane seat

241 'Strip Chair and Table', 1974;
chairs are made of six 11 ($4\frac{3}{8}$")
strips bent to form legs, seat and
back, suitable for stacking, also
available with arms; laminated
wood with ash veneer in natural,
white or black finish; table
90 × 90, 120 × 85, 120 × 120,
170 × 85 (2'11" × 2'11",
3'11" × 2'9$\frac{1}{2}$", 3'11 × 3'11",
5'7" × 2'9$\frac{1}{2}$")

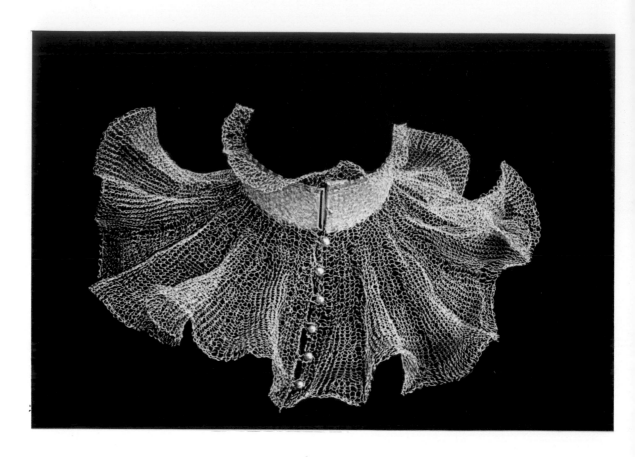

242 Collar, 1975; knitted from fine
silver and 18 ct. gold wire; 45.6
(18")
Designed and made by Arline M
Fisch, USA

243 'Glass Environment' Free
form, hot tooled glass
Made by André Bellici, USA

244, 245 Two Bowls, 1977; coiled
stoneware and coloured porc-
elain, glazed interior; 30 × 25
(1′ × 10″)
Made by Lene Regius, Denmark

246 Adjustable Music Stand;
walnut and cherry; 1.17 × 1.78
(3′10″ × 5′10″) high

247 'Wish-bone Chair';
mahogany with woven leather
webbing seat
Both designed and made by
Espenet, USA

248 Glass container for the tea
ceremony; mould blown, with
gold and silver foil decoration;
finished on the grinding weel to
obtain a perfect fit
Made by Kyohei Fujita, Japan

249 Round vase with cased pat-
tern cut out of fibre glass fabric
Made by Benny Motzfeldt,
Norway

250 Bowl, 1976; bull oak, 15 × 25
(6″ × 10″)

251 Screen, 1974; cedar
1.98 × 2.44m long (6′6″ × 8′ long)

The creator of the pieces on these pages, Stephen Hogbin of Canada, believes that craft is the contact between art and technology. Technology aims to supply the 'average' person's basic needs, a concept now increasingly in question, but a craftsman can supply something more personal. The wooden bowls and bird table clearly illustrate the potential of his special turning/carving technique. Using a milling machine, originally devised to make a screen for the Metropolitan Toronto Library, he carves individual pieces, often in close contact with one particular client. For the last three years, he has been interested in creating pieces to support 'cultural myths' such as the rituals involved in eating. He believes in the symbolism of objects; the fact that functional objects reflect the society which created them. This perceived symbolism is then worked into the wooden artefact in question.

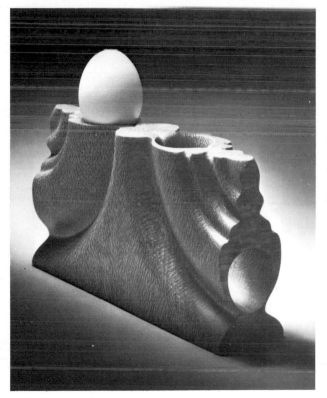

252 'Bird' table, 1976; yellow walnut, 27 × 90 (11″ × 3′)

253 Egg-cup; silky brown oak, 11 × 21 × 5 (4″ × 8″ × 2″)

254 Plate, 1977; white pine, 64 (2′1″)

255 Bowl, 1977; black cherry, 40
(16")
Designed and made by Stephen
Hogbin, Canada

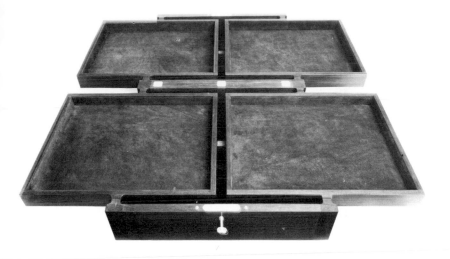

256 Jewelry Display Box, 1978; when locked the box contains four trays stacked vertically; to display the contents, the lid is fully opened and the trays lifted out. Four sections are then removed from the sides of the box and two cental pegs, neatly hidden in the base, are inserted as illustrated; the trays can now be put back into the box forming a horizontal display, with each tray held in place by three small brass dowels; Indian rosewood with brass fittings and dark brown suede lining
Designed and made by Desmond Ryan, England

257 'Butterfly and Bees' necklace, 1974; 18 ct. gold, ivory, mother-of-pearl, shell, transparent glass beads, pink silk

Using mainly gold in conjunction with precious stones such as emeralds and diamonds; semi-precious quarts, seed pearls and ivory, and non-precious shells and glass beads, Jacqueline Mina creates jewelry with a sense of timelessness. Each piece is unique and is worked spontaneously, purely by hand, in an attempt to allow the form to develop sub-consciously. She produces numerous drawings in order to explore new ideas and resolve technical problems, but precise working drawings are never necessary. The fact that she studied embroidery is reflected in the richness of her earlier work, such as the 'Butterfly and Bees' necklace, through the use of intri-cately woven chains and the working of the gold till it almost resembles material. The later jewellery shows a development towards a greater simplicity of line, but inspiration continues to be drawn from natural forms. Movement plays an important part in these pieces, something impossible to capture in a photo-graph. The jewellery is designed to be worn, to be seen moving. Her characteristic undulating line symbolizes this movement; to her it is like hair, moving water, the edge of a leaf, or the vibration of light

photography: David Cripps

178

258 Necklace, 1978; 18 ct. gold
with emerald beads, carved pink
tourmalines and marquise
diamonds

259 Pendant and Earrings, 1975;
18 ct. gold with seed pearls and
agate
All designed and made by
Jacqueline Mina, England
*Courtesy of Argenta Gallery,
London*

260 'Migration over Lapland';
tapestry, 1975–76 handspun linen
and wool, birch bark, sisal
5.6 × 2.7m (18'4" × 8'10")
Designed and made by Jane
Balsgaard, Denmark

Architects, Designers, Manufacturers

Tadao Ando Architects and
Associates
6-F Domus Building
5-chome, 8 Minamihonmachi
Higashi-ku
Osaka 541
Japan

Argenta Gallery
82 Fulham Rd
London SW3
England

Jane Balsgaard
Lille Strandstraede 15
1254 Copenhagen
Denmark

André Bellici
Thurston Studio
RD1 Campbell NY 14821
USA

T P Bennett & Son
Architects and Planning
Consultants
262 High Holborn
London WC1
England

Karen Bennicke
Bregentved Gl. Smedie
4690 Haslev
Denmark

Giancarlo Bicocchi
Luigi Bicocchi
Roberto Monsani Architetti
Lungarno A Vespucci 18
50123 Florence
Italy

Daniele Boatti
via Gesú 8
Milan
Italy

Claus Bonderup Architect
Urbansgade 19
9000 Halborg
Denmark

Castelijn meubelen B V
Zuidweg 11c
Ripjpwetering
The Netherlands

Wendell Castle
18 Maple St
Scottsville NY 14546
USA

Brian Clarke
c/o Decorative Art
35 Red Lion Square
London WC1R 4SG

Kamran Diba Architect
c/o Decorative Art
35 Red Lion Square
London WC1R 4SG
England

Nanna Ditzel Design Office
Interspace
Rosemont Rd
London NW3

Espenet
Star Route
Bolinas, California
USA

Arline M Fisch
4316 Arcadia Drive
San Diego, Ca 92103
USA

Kenji Fujimura
Kyoto Design House
Kyoto
Japan

Kyohei Fujita
President of Japan Art Glass
Craft Association
Itchikawa
Japan

Giovannetti SpA
52145 Bottegone (Pistoia)
Italy

GMW Partnership
17 Manchester Square
London W1
England

George J Haefeli
16 rue du Nord
CH-2300 La Chaux-de-Fonds
Switzerland

Bente Hansen
Mosevangen 48
3460 Birkerød
Denmark

Anthony Hawksley
Tredorwin
Nancledra, Penzance
Cornwall
England

Stephen Hogbin
Route 1
Caledon East
Ontario
Canada

Michael and Patricia Hopkins
49a Devonshire Hill
London NW3 1NX
England

Richard Kjaergard
Gadevangen 7A
2800 Lyngby
Denmark

Masayuki Kurokawa Architect &
Associates
Flat Hoyama 101
5-15-9 Minami-Aoyama
Minato-ku
Tokyo

L C P Trim Ltd
Waterfall Lane
Cradley Heath
Warley, West Midland B64 6QA
England

Wendell Lovett Architect
1445 Southeast 55th St
Bellevue
Washington 98006
USA

Finn Lynggaard
Adalsvej 40
1970 Hørsholm
Denmark

Jaqueline Mina
5 Pope's Grove
Twickenham Middlesex
England

William Morgan Architects
220 East Forsyth St
Jacksonville, Florida 32202
USA

Benny Motzfeldt
Drammensveien
Oslo 2
Norway

Antoine Predock Architect
300 12th St NW
Albuquerque, New Mexico
USA

David Pye
Regency House
Downgate
Tidebrook
Wadhurst, Sussex
England

Lene Regius
Mysselhojgard Gl. Lejre
4320 Lejre
Denmark

Patrick Reyntiens
Burleighfield Lodge
Loudwater Nr High Wycombe
Buckinghamshire
England

Desmond Ryan
Hayle Mill
Tovil
Maidstone, Kent
England

Ludwig Schaffrath
511 Alsdorf-Ofden
Theodor-Seipp-Str 118
West Germany

Johannes Schreiter
c/o Decorative Art
35 Red Lion Square
London WC1R 4SG

Helmut Schulitz
Germaniastrasse 30
8000 Munich 40
West Germany

Walter Seelig
c/o The Hadler Galleries
35–37 East 20th St
10003 New York
USA

Jean Sonnier and Dominique
Ronsseray
5 rue Lalo
75116 Paris
France

Studio PER
Caspe 151
Barcelona 13
Spain

Timo & Tuomo Suomalainen
Architects
Itäranta 7
02100 Espoo 10
Finland

Stanley Tigerman & Associates
233 North Michigan Ave
Chicago Illinois 60601
USA

Inger Thing
Dronningeengen 9
2950 Vedbaek
Denmark

Shigeru Uchida Design Office
1–7–14 Minami Aoyama
Minato-ku
Tokyo

Vetreria Vistosi
San vio 866
30123 Venice
Italy

Dick Weiss
811 N 36th St
Seattle, Washington 98103
USA

Rupert Williamson
5 Goddard Croft
Greenleys, Milton Keynes
England

Shoei Yoh
Yoh Design Office
1–12–30 Heiwa
Minami-ku
Fukuoka-shi

Pierre Zoelly
Dufourstrasse 7
CH-8702 Zollikon-Zürich
Switzerland